THE ROMAN TRIUMVIRATES

CHARLES MERIVALE

Published by Left of Brain Books

Copyright © 2021 Left of Brain Books

ISBN 978-1-396-31931-0

First Edition

All rights reserved. No part of this publication may be reproduced, distributed, or transmitted in any form or by any means, including photocopying, recording, or other electronic or mechanical methods, without the prior written permission of the publisher, except in the case of brief quotations embodied in critical reviews and certain other noncommercial uses permitted by copyright law. Left of Brain Books is a division of Left of Brain Onboarding Pty Ltd.

Table of Contents

CHAPTER I. (U.C. 583. B.C. 71.—U.C. 687. B.C. 67.)
The Reaction Against Sulla's Legislation. —Rise of Pompeius.   1

CHAPTER II. (U.C. 684. B.C. 70.—U.C. 692. B.C. 62.)
Ascendency of Pompeius.—His Subjugation of the Cilician Pirates, and Conquests in the East.   18

CHAPTER III. (U.C. 691. B.C. 63.—U.C. 694. B.C. 60.)
State of Parties in the City.—Consulship of Cicero, and Conspiracy of Catilina.   33

CHAPTER IV. (U.C. 693. B.C. 61.—U.C. 697. B.C. 57.)
The First Triumvirate of Cæsar, Pompeius, and Crassus.   52

CHAPTER V. (U.C. 696. B.C. 58.—U.C. 703. B.C. 51.)
Cæsar's Conquest of Gaul.—Death of Crassus and Dissolution of the First Triumvirate.   67

CHAPTER VI. (U.C. 703. B.C. 51.—U.C. 705. B.C. 49.)
Rupture Between Cæsar and the Senate.   85

CHAPTER VII. (U.C. 705. B.C. 50.—U.C. 708. B.C. 46.)
The Civil War.—Battle of Pharsalia.—Death of Pompeius.—Death of Cato.   101

CHAPTER VIII. (U.C. 709. B.C. 45.—U.C. 710. B.C. 44.)
Tyranny and Death of Cæsar.   122

CHAPTER IX. (U.C.710. B.C. 44.) Caius Octavius Succeeds to the Inheritance of Julius Cæsar.   138

CHAPTER X. (U.C. 710. B.C. 44.—U.C. 712. B.C. 42)
The Second Triumvirate: Octavius, Antonius, and Lepidus.   147

CHAPTER XI. (U.C. 712. B.C. 42.)
Last Effort of the Republicans: the Battle of Philippi.   160

CHAPTER XII. U.C. 712. B.C. 42.—U.C. 724. B.C. 30.
Contest Between Octavius and Antonius.—Battle of Actium.—Octavius Becomes Master of the State.   166

CHAPTER I.
(U.C. 583. B.C. 71.—U.C. 687. B.C. 67.)

THE REACTION AGAINST SULLA'S LEGISLATION.— RISE OF POMPEIUS.

Working of the Roman republican constitution.

THE Roman republic maintained itself for a period of nearly five hundred years; and this has been commonly regarded as a striking instance of the vitality of free institutions. But such an idea can only be admitted with much abatement. The polity of the conquering city was in fact ill-fitted for duration, for it was essentially the government of the many by the few, of a commonalty by a nobility, of an unarmed multitude by an armed order, of subjects in many lands by their victors in one central position. It was only by the happy circumstances under which the lower classes were from time to time elevated, in spite of all resistance, into the ranks of the governors, that this inequality was not redressed by violence, and the commonwealth overthrown by revolution. It was only by the occasional suppression of the free state, and the creation of a temporary dictator, that the balance of power was at many a critical moment maintained.

Results of the Punic and Social wars.

When the conquering race at Rome had made itself master of Italy, and a single state held sway over a number of subject communities, the time was almost come for the appointment of a permanent ruler. Probably the rivalry of Carthage and the invasion of Hannibal, by drawing all classes at Rome, and most of her allies and dependents, more closely together, postponed the inevitable event. After the fall of Hannibal and Carthage the ascendency of the Scipios, first in war, first in peace, first in the hearts of their countrymen, seemed to point more clearly to such a solution. Once more the wars in the East, and the brilliant conquests of Greece and Asia, diverted men's thoughts to new aspirations, and the era of monarchy was not yet. Under the Gracchi the spirit of impending monarchy again loomed visibly; again the struggle of the Social War averted the consummation. From this time the Roman constitution was proved to be impracticable. It would not work. The sovereign power was disputed openly between the leaders of two rival armies, who barely deigned to avow themselves the heads of two domestic parties.

Monarchial power of Sulla.

When Sulla gained the ascendency, he made himself a king under the title of perpetual dictator. He resigned this power, indeed, but he had not the less made it his own. It was his singular ambition to re-establish the free state by personal caprice and open force, and to found a republican constitution upon a monarchical revolution. He failed. The fabric he set up was a mere shadow, which hardly for a moment disguised the fact that the real government of Rome must henceforth rest in the hands of her strongest citizen. The history of the Roman Triumvirates is the history of the brief interval during which this shadow of a free state still hovered before men's eyes, while the permanent establishment of imperial sovereignty was only delayed by the nearly equal forces of the chiefs who contended for it. Sixteen years after the death of Sulla the government was virtually shared between three military rulers, who formed what has been called the First Triumvirate. Seventeen years later a similar compact was renewed, and more definite powers were assumed, by a second Triumvirate. Thirteen years later the commonwealth of Rome had fallen actually under the sway of a single despot, who styled himself emperor. The period of which the following chapters treat comprises forty-six years, from the death of Sulla to the crowning victory of Augustus.

Sulla and the Roman aristocracy.

Sulla could have given no greater proof of confidence in the stability of his work than by abdicating his personal power, and leaving the commonwealth to be guided by the political principles he had established. He believed that an oligarchy of wealth and station could govern Rome, and maintain the position in which he had replaced it. It was sufficient in his view to launch the *Optimates*, the self-styled best or noblest, of the city freely on the career which he had opened for them, by suppressing the rival powers of the tribunate, and making them supreme in the comitia, unchecked in the administration of the provinces, and commanders of the national armies. He was not aware that in fact the authority which he had exercised had depended solely on his own personal ability, and that the aristocracy had no vital force of its own to make use of the high position he had regained for it. It had indeed no hold upon the nation, no confidence in itself; it was at the moment singularly deficient in men of commanding eminence. It had in fact survived its vital powers, and the forces which had grown up around it both in the city and the provinces had already passed beyond its proper control. Sulla was himself a man of extraordinary genius. He had been hacked by an irresistible military force, and he had encountered the popular party at a moment when it was demoralized by its own bloody excesses. But it was only under these exceptional circumstances that the aristocracy had gained a transient success. It was unable to maintain its vantage ground. The abdication of Sulla may have hastened its fall, but the fall was from the first inevitable.

Sulla's idea of his own work.

The great dictator had relied also upon the principles of Roman polity, which he considered himself to have re-established. Sulla was not the last, nor, perhaps, was he the first of the Romans who imagined that he could restore the commonwealth, and replace it upon a lasting foundation, by arresting its natural course of development, and forcing it back into the channel which had proved too narrow for it. He dreamt that the provinces, now widely extended through three continents, peopled by numerous colonies of Roman extraction, teeming with the interests of a multitude of Roman citizens engaged in every branch of art and commerce, could be held in hand by an official oligarchy of public men, as in the old days when the dominions of the republic were all comprised within a circle of a few days' journey from the city. His thoughts reverted to the period when the plebeians of Rome were really inferior in rank and power to the patricians, when they were regarded and treated as of lower origin, and their pretensions to equal privileges scouted with disdain. He would deny them the protection of their tribunes now, when they had become substantially the ruling power in the state, and it was through the tribunes that their power was exercised. Sulla was a fanatic. He believed in his own good fortune; he believed in the fortune of Rome. He was ready to pit Rome and himself against the world. He entertained no doubt that Rome, restored to the political condition in which, in his view, she had been most prosperous, and restored under his own victorious auspices, was destined to control all the changes of circumstance around her, and rise triumphant over every foreign or domestic enemy. The notion that Sulla resigned his power in petulance, or in despair of establishing the reactionary policy to which he had devoted himself, seems to be founded in an entire misconception of his character. He was a fanatic, and he abdicated in sublime complacency at the enduring success which he fully believed himself to have achieved.

Results of Sulla's career.

The work effected by the great dictator did in fact lay the foundation of the long civil wars and the political revolutions which followed.

Effects of Roman conquests.

1. The definite establishment of the Roman power throughout Greece and Macedonia and a great part of Asia Minor, by the victories of their great military leader, rendered it necessary to maintain a large standing army permanently quartered at a distance from the capital. This mercenary force could only be held by one paramount commander, and to this generalissimo it was necessary to entrust the appointment of every subordinate officer, the power of making war or peace along an immense frontier, the levying of contributions from a vast array of provinces and of dependent states, and to allow him to prolong his command from year to year almost without reference to his legitimate masters in the city. The transfer of such a command from one pro-consul to another, accompanied by the displacement of a horde of servants and clients, the

frustration of sanguine hopes, the excitement of irregular ambitions, was in itself a revolution, and could hardly fail to lead to a civil war.

Results of the extension of the franchise.

2. The progress of events had hitherto tended towards the enfranchisement of the provinces, and the assimilation of the subjects of the city to her native citizens. The Social War had resulted in the admission of the free population of all Italy to the civil rights of the Romans. A precedent had been set which could not fail to be followed, and which must eventually lead to the incorporation of the whole mass of provincials in one political body. The right indeed of voting at the elections of magistrates was still practically restricted to the citizens who resided at the centre of affairs, for there was no more sacred principle among the Romans than that of confining all civil transactions to the very spot on which the auspices could be taken, which was itself at the centre of the city. But the Roman franchise entitled its possessor to a share in the functions of general administration. It was slowly and gradually that the Italians and other foreign citizens obtained a footing on the ladder of civic honors; but under the command of the Roman Proconsul and Imperator they engrossed a large part of the military appointments throughout the provinces, together with all the fiscal employments. The knights, whether of Roman or Italian origin, became largely interested in commerce, and settled abroad in the pursuit of wealth, placing their local knowledge and their capital at the service of the government in the farming of its revenues and management of its resources. Not only were the provincials thus placed at the mercy of the military establishment of their conquerors, but all the most lucrative employments among them were seized by financial agents of the central government. Roman Citizens fastened themselves upon every limb of the great body of the empire, and sucked its blood at every pore. It only remained to secure the fruits of these exclusive privileges, and to invest the enjoyment of them with practical irresponsibility. When the provinces complained of the oppressions under which they suffered, they found indeed ready ears among the rival parties in the state. Every pro-consul and every subordinate agent abroad had his personal enemies at home, who were prepared to listen to the charges which the sufferers made against them. The great object of the class of

Optimates was to secure to themselves the administration of justice in the city, and confine the appointment of judges, in cases of provincial malversation, to men of the senatorial order. The commons, on the other hand, represented for the most part by the Equites, or horsemen, the bulk of whom ranked with the plebeians, contended for a share in these offices; and one of the most constant and vital contests of classes within the city for many years was whether the *judicia* should be confined to the senators or extended to the knights also. Sulla had excluded the lower order from any place in this important department of administration. But the provincials chafed under the ascendency of the Optimates, as that from which they had hitherto suffered most sensibly. They were disposed to lend their weight to any movement in favor of the plebeian faction at home, which they regarded as more favorable to their interests, as less rigid and exclusive in its ideas of government, as imbued on the whole with the principles of a cosmopolitan policy, and which led them to indulge at least in some indefinite hopes of future advantage to themselves. The leaders of the popular party at Rome had always shown themselves more inclined to favor and employ them than their rivals. The popular party had itself owed its rise to more liberal principles of government, and as the aristocrats exhibited under Sulla's supremacy a narrower and more selfish spirit than ever, so did the democrats rally round themselves all the classes at home and abroad which aspired to a fuller enjoyment of Roman privileges and advantages.

Growth of a military order.

3. But under the fair surface of a polity of ranks and classes, there had now grown up a power almost independent of nobles and commons, of Romans and provincials. The real control of government rested with the army. In the conduct of her distant and incessant wars, the republic of the Scipios and the Gracchi had created an instrument which had become too strong for civil restraints at the hands either of the senate or of the popular assemblies. The ancient military constitution of Rome had rested on the annual enlistment of all its able-bodied citizens for the defence of its frontier against enemies who lay almost beneath its walls. The Roman legions were a militia enrolled practically for home service only. Their annual campaigns lasted for a few

months, after which the soldier-citizen returned to his farm or his counter, and received there the solicitations of candidates for the next elections. The long wars of Italy, in which the Roman people had contended against the Gauls, the Samnites, and the Etruscans, against Hannibal and Pyrrhus, against the united forces of the Italian nations, had compelled their government to enlist its citizens for a term of years. The legionary had long ceased to exercise his vote in the Campus, and had come to disregard his civil functions as a citizen, while he looked to the profession of arms as the road to emoluments and honors, as the object of his pride and interest. He had already become a source of danger to the civil government, when the progress of his conquests removed him to distant shores and while this distance alienated him more and more from his native land, it deprived him at least of any immediate means of affronting and injuring her.

Roman jealousy of provincials.

As long, indeed, as the legions continued to be supplied by recruits drawn from Rome herself, or even from the Roman colonies in Italy or the neighboring provinces, the metropolis might rely with some confidence on the deep-rooted attachment of her people, and on the principles of domestic obedience which the genuine citizen could not without difficulty shake off, however far removed from her, however long disused to her control. He still prided himself on his connection with the ruling race, and still regarded himself as a being of a higher order than the Italian or the provincial who served as an auxiliary in the cohorts that fought beside him.

Character of the Roman legionaries.

This feeling of pride Marius had materially weakened by destroying the distinction of classes, and calling upon the proletarians from the lowest order of the state to assist in her conquests. From the time of the exhausting wars against the Cimbri and the Teutones, the Roman soldier had ceased to represent the aristocracy of Rome, and to share its prejudices. He had no stake in his own country; he was a man without a country, which, among the settled communities of the ancient world, was regarded as something strange and portentous. And so, indeed, it was a portent of change and revolution, of violence and rapine. The Roman legionary, thus drawn from the dregs of the populace, and quartered through the best years of his life in Greece and Asia, in Spain and Gaul, lived solely upon his pay, enhanced by extortion or plunder. His thirst of rapine grew upon him. He required his chiefs to indulge him with the spoil of cities and provinces; and when a foreign enemy was not at hand, he was tempted to turn against the subjects of the state, or, if need be, against the state itself. The regular military chest was too quickly exhausted by the ordinary expenses of the military establishment. Often the troops could not even be brought into the field except by the sacrifice of some helpless community, against which a quarrel was picked for no other purpose but to enable the Imperator to mobilize his legions. But no prey was so glittering as Italy and Rome itself; and towards their own native shores the eyes of the greedy legionaries were now too frequently directed, while their chiefs were themselves equally eager to strike at the centre of government for the highest prizes which the republic could bestow. Marius and Sulla, Cinna and Carbo had led the forces of Rome against Rome herself, in the predatory spirit of the Cimbri and the Teutones before, of the Goths and the Vandals some centuries afterwards. Rome, at the very height of her material power, in the full career of her foreign conquests, lay as completely at the mercy of the true barbarians of that age as when she was helpless to avert the inroads of an Alaric or an Attila.

Early career of Pompeius surnamed the Great.

The problem which thus presented itself to the minds of patriots—how, namely, to avert the impending dissolution of their polity under the blows of their own defenders—was indeed an anxious and might well appear a hopeless one. It was to the legions only that they could trust, and the legions were notoriously devoted to their chiefs, to whom, indeed, they had sworn the military oath, rather than to the civil administration and principles of law, in which they could take no interest. The triumph of Sulla had been secured by the accession to his side of Pompeius Strabo, the commander of a large force quartered in Italy. These troops had transferred their obedience to a younger Pompeius, the son of their late leader. Under his auspices they had gained many victories; they had put down the Marian faction, headed by Carbo, in

Sicily, and had finally secured the ascendency of the senate on the shores of Africa. Sulla had evinced some jealousy of their captain, who was young in years, and as yet had not risen above the rank of Eques; but when Pompeius led his victorious legions back to Italy, the people rose in the greatest enthusiasm to welcome him, and the dictator, yielding to their impetuosity, had granted him a triumph and hailed him with the title of "Magnus." Young as he was, he became at once, on the abdication of Sulla, the greatest power in the commonwealth. This he soon caused to be known and felt.

The Consulship of Catulus and Lepidus.

The lead of the senatorial party had now fallen to Q. Lutatius Catulus and M. Æmilius Lepidus, the heads of two of the oldest and noblest families of Rome. The election of these chiefs to the consulship for the year 676 of the city (B.C. 78) seemed to secure for a time the ascendency of the nobles, and the maintenance of Sulla's oligarchical constitution bequeathed to their care. The death of the retired dictator, which occurred in the course of the same year, was felt perhaps as a relief by the party which he had oppressed with his protection. But there were divisions within the party itself which seemed to seize the opportunity for breaking forth. Lepidus was inflamed with ambition to create a faction of his own, and imitate the career of the usurpers before him. He had served as an officer under Sulla, and had attached to himself a portion of the army. His marriage with a daughter of the tribune, Saturninus, had connected him with the party of Marius. He had formed relations with the young Pompeius, through whose influence he had acquired the consulship, but whose power he now affected to slight. On the death of Sulla he had spoken disparagingly of the dictator's services, and threatened to tamper with his enactments. But he had miscalculated his strength. Pompeius disavowed him, and lent the weight of his popularity and power to the support of Catulus; and the senate hoped to avert an outbreak by engaging both the consuls by an oath to abstain from assailing each other. During the remainder of his term of office Lepidus refrained from action but as soon as he reached his province, the Narbonensis in Gaul, he developed his plans, summoned to his standard the Marians, who had taken refuge in great numbers in that region, and invoked the aid of the Italians, with the promise of restoring to them the lands of which they had been dispossessed by Sulla's veterans. With the aid of M. Junius Brutus, who commanded in the Cisalpine, he made an inroad into Etruria, and called upon the remnant of its people, who had been decimated by Sulla, to rise against the faction of their oppressors. The senate, now thoroughly alarmed, charged Catulus with its defence; the veterans, restless and dissatisfied with their fields and farms, crowded to the standard of Pompeius. Two Roman armies met near the Milvian bridge, a few miles to the north of the city, and Lepidus received a check, which was again and again repeated, till he was driven to flee into Sardinia, and there perished shortly afterwards of fever. Pompeius pursued Brutus into the Cisalpine; but the senate was satisfied with the defeat and death of the first movers of the revolt, and abstained from vindictive measures against their followers. The counsels of Catulus, one of the most honorable of the Roman leaders, were always moderate and magnanimous.

Death of Lepidus.

The temper of Lepidus, on the other hand, had been vain and selfish. He betrayed the party from which he had sprung, and violated the oath he had taken to it. His birth and station had inspired him with empty hopes, which he had neither talents nor influence to realize. His enterprise was feeble and ill-concerted, and seems to have been precipitated by petulant vexation at the resistance of the senate. The wariest of the Marian faction refrained from entangling themselves in it. Their cause lost nothing by his death. The remnant of his troops was carried over to Spain by Perperna, and there swelled the forces of an abler leader of the same party, Q. Sertorius.

Sertorius in Spain.

This chief, by birth a Sabine, had served under Marius against the Cimbri, and in later campaigns in Spain had made himself popular with the natives of that province. He had kept himself free from the stain of the proscriptions, and this was now held as a merit by both the rival parties in the state. On the triumph of Sulla he had retired from Italy, and while he despaired of restoring the fortunes of the Marians at home, had sought to fortify an asylum for them among the yet untamed inhabitants of the western peninsula. The Iberians flocked around him with vague aspirations; but Sulla sent his lieutenant, Annius, in pursuit of him, and drove him across the sea into Mauretania. As the brave but unsuccessful champion of a long depressed cause, Sertorius assumed a somewhat mythical character in the traditions of his party. It was currently reported that despairing of the fortunes of the Marian faction, he had meditated a retreat to the "Islands of the Blest," in the bosom of the Atlantic. But, in fact, he was driven to no such extremity. Making himself allies among the people of Africa, be defeated the Roman army under one of Sulla's lieutenants. The Lusitanians summoned him again to their aid; the western tribes of the peninsula rose and flocked to his standard. The Sullan party in Spain were commanded by Metellus, a weak and irresolute leader; the dictator's abdication and death discouraged his followers. Meanwhile Sertorius acted with promptness and vigor. Again and again he routed his opponents. He proclaimed the independence of the Iberian people, and organized a free state among them, with an originality of conception to which Roman history offers no parallel. If our accounts are to be trusted, he conceived the bold idea of educating the youth of Spain in the manners of the Romans, and constituting a rival republic in the west, to balance the conquests of his countrymen beyond the Adriatic. But the spirit of Italy, if not of Rome, was still, it seems, too strongly rooted in his breast for so monstrous a treason. When Pompeius arrived, bringing with him a strong reinforcement of exiles from Italy, his plans insensibly changed. He regarded himself once more as the head of a national party; he placed the interests of his Marian followers in the foreground, and treated the natives of the land as allies or subjects. When Mithridates sought to concert with him a combined attack upon the centre of the Roman government from the east and from the west, proposing the alliance, as he said, of a new Pyrrhus with a new Hannibal, no child of a ruling race, no lord of human kind, could brook a union so shocking, and he declared that he would never suffer a barbarian to set foot on Roman soil.

Death of Sertorius and its consequences.

Such at least was the legend of Sertorius in the imagination of his Roman followers. The new chief of the Marians stood in need of all the aid they could give, of all the glory with which they could encircle him. The senate took the full measure of his prowess, and sent their brave young general, Pompeius, to replace the worn-out veteran, Metellus. Yet Pompeius found the encounter both difficult and hazardous. He contended with Sertorius in many engagements, in one of which, on the banks of the Sucro, he would have suffered grave disaster but for the opportune assistance of Metellus. Pompeius was reduced to act on the defensive, while he called upon the senate for ampler succors. In this strait he was relieved more by the defects of his opponent's policy than by any vigor or ability of his own. Sertorius, it seems, became inflated with the glory of his unexpected successes. He began to despise the simple people whom he had deceived by pretending to supernatural powers, training a milk-white hind to follow him, and affecting to consult it as a familiar spirit. When his Roman followers quarrelled with their Spanish auxiliaries, he sacrificed his new to his older adherents, and even permitted the massacre of the children of their chiefs, whom he had kept as hostages under pretence of educating them. From this time there was no union between the diverse elements of his power; he enjoyed no security even from the intrigues of his Roman lieutenants. Perperna raised a mutiny in his camp, and effected his assassination. But this upstart lacked ability to maintain the post he had seized. Pompeius, with fresh forces, resumed the attack, speedily overcame his adversary, and put him to death. The chief of the senatorial party now filled the province with his steadiest adherents, and organized the peninsula as a fortress of the Roman oligarchy. Returning to the city through the south of Gaul, he confirmed the Narbonensis and the Provincia in their allegiance to the same dominant faction, and secured to its interests the whole of the Roman dominions in the west. The senate exulted in the solid conquest which it had thus effected, and accorded to its champion, yet young and unennobled, the honor of a triumph, in which Metellus was allowed to participate, as a tribute to his rank rather than as a reward for his services.

The Servile War of Spartacus.

Pompeius had thus recovered a great province for the republic at the moment when it seemed on the point of being lost through the inefficiency of one of the senatorial chiefs. Another leader of the dominant party was about to yield him another victory. A war was raging in the heart of Italy. A body of gladiators had broken away from their confinement at Capua under the lead of Spartacus, a Thracian captive, had seized a large quantity of arms, and had made themselves a retreat or place of defence in the crater of Mount Vesuvius. There they had gathered around them the fugitive slaves and banditti of the district, and had assumed an attitude of open defiance to the government. The troops of the republic had been directed against them; they had defeated the prætor, C. Clodius, and strengthened themselves with additional succors. The veterans of Sulla, quartered in central Italy, were restless, and threatened to quit the farms, of which they were weary, and rush to the plunder of the cities. In the course of three years the forces of Spartacus had increased to 40,000 or, according to some writers, even to 100,000 men. He had sacked some of the principal places in Campania, and rendered himself virtually master of the southern half of the peninsula. But the native races of Italy shrank from the contact of slaves and brigands; and when he found that he could not raise a national revolt against Rome, he knew that his cause was desperate, and exhorted his followers to employ all their strength in bursting the barrier of the Alps, and dispersing themselves among the northern provinces, from which they had been for the most part drawn. Meanwhile his tumultuous bands were intoxicated with their successes and ravenous for further plunder. They continued to ravage the country on all sides. The consuls were directed to lead the legions against them, but were ignominiously defeated. In the absence of Pompeius in Spain and of Lucullus in the East, M. Crassus was the most prominent among the chiefs of the party in power. This illustrious noble was a man of great influence, acquired more by his wealth, for which he obtained the surname of Dives, than for any marked ability in the field or in the forum but he had a large following of clients and dependents, who helped to raise him to the first place in the city, and who now swelled the cry for placing a powerful force under his orders, and entrusting to his hands the deliverance of Italy. The brigands themselves were becoming demoralized by lack of discipline. Crassus drove them before him to the extremity of the peninsula. At Rhegium they bargained with a fleet of Cilician pirates for a passage into Sicily, but they were betrayed and disappointed by these treacherous allies, and Spartacus could only save a remnant of them by furiously breaking through the lines of his assailants. This brave gladiator was still formidable, and it was feared that Rome itself might be exposed to his desperate attack. The senate sent importunate messages to recall both Pompeius and Lucullus to its defence. Crassus, on his part, bitterly regretting the supineness with which he had suffered the enemy to escape from his own hands to fall into the hands of his rivals, exerted himself to anticipate their return. He confined Spartacus to the mountains, but was still unable to reduce him. The conqueror of Sertorius had completed the pacification of Spain; he hastened back to Italy, traversed the country with speed, and took from Crassus the forces with which he had failed to secure the victory. Spartacus had now become an easy prey, and the laurels were quickly won with which Pompeius was honored by his partial countrymen. Crassus was deeply mortified, and the senate itself might feel some alarm at the redoubled triumphs of a champion of whose loyalty it was not secure.

The Mithridatic war.

But the senatorial party had yet another leader, and a man of more ability than Crassus, at the head of another army. The authority of Pompeius in the western provinces was balanced in the East by that of L. Licinius Lucullus, who commanded the forces of the republic in the struggle which she was still maintaining against Mithridates. The power of Rome both in Greece and Asia had been in jeopardy for many years under the attacks with which it had been assailed by the brave and politic king of Pontus. Stunned by the blows he had received from Sulla, this indomitable Asiatic had risen again and defied the valor and discipline of the legions. But the existence of so formidable an enemy had furnished the senate with an excuse for maintaining an immense force in the eastern provinces, and putting it under the command of the ablest general it could select from its own ranks, to be a bulwark of his party as well as of the commonwealth. Lucullus, who had been deputed to this important post, was held in high repute as an officer, at the same time that his wealth, birth, and talents gave him an eminent position in civil affairs. He had obtained the consulship in the year 74, during the progress of the war with Sertorius. He had quitted the city when the tribunes, with the support of the other consul, Cotta, were moving the abrogation of the Sullan (or Cornelian) laws, and had undertaken the command of the large army which Sulla had left in the East as an instrument for maintaining the ascendency of the oligarchical government. Lucullus was faithful to his party, but he was content to serve its interests at a distance from the centre of civil strife. He was well acquainted with the theatre of events in the East, having acted as an officer under Sulla in some previous campaigns, and having distinguished himself for activity and military prowess. He had then followed his chief to Rome, but had arrived there after the era of the proscriptions, so that his popularity with the citizens was not affected by the stain of bloodshed. He was a man of refined tastes, which had suffered no debasement from the rude manners of the camp. He professed a taste for letters, and cultivated the Greek manners, which, in a few superior natures at least, were beginning to elevate the Roman Character to its highest pitch of combined gracefulness and vigor. In every respect Lucullus was worthy to assume the chief place in the direction of the senatorial party, and it might be expected that, by the command of the most powerful division of the national armies, he would secure to that party the continuance of its authority.

Defeat of Mithridates.

The military successes of Lucullus fully justified the choice of the government. Mithridates had recovered from the check he had recently received; and though his advances for aid to Tigranes, the powerful king of Armenia, met with a cold reception, he had been enabled to recruit his forces and carry his arms through the regions of Bithynia and Phrygia, and had encamped before Chalcedon, opposite to the coast of Thrace. Here he was besieging the Roman general Cotta; and though his troops were, for the most part, commanded by Greek officers, he was ill-provided with the materials or the skill for reducing a well-fortified and well-defended citadel. Lucullus, relinquishing the easy task of overrunning the provinces which the invader had left behind him, determined to succor the garrisons still in his front, and succeeded, by skilful and cautious manœuvres, in reducing the cumbrous host of his opponent to straits by famine, while he refused to encounter it in open battle. Chalcedon was relieved; Mithridates withdrew from before it, but only to make another attack upon the stronghold of Cyzicus. Here again Lucullus adopted his previous tactics, and here, too, he compelled the enemy to abandon his position after suffering severe losses. The king of Pontus effected his own escape by sea, leaving his army to be harassed and finally routed. He was now driven to take refuge with the king of Armenia. Thither Lucullus followed him, but not till he had devoted himself to the restoration of the Roman power throughout the Lesser Asia, and had placed the inhabitants under a milder rule than that which they had lately endured at the hands of the Roman officials. He was animated by an honest sense of justice, and the check he put upon the fiscal tyranny of the government made him many enemies both in the province and in the city. The senate began to find that however successful their general might be in the field, his civil administration was calculated to weaken rather than to confirm their ascendency. At the same time, the party of the knights and of the commons was steadily regaining its due weight in the counsels of the re public. The people, encouraged underhand by Pompeius, by Crassus, and by other chiefs in whom the senate had hitherto confided, were bent upon restoring the powers of the tribunate, and overthrowing the institutions of the late dictator. The support which the senate now gave to Lucullus was more lukewarm than at first; but he had by this time established his authority throughout the province, and continued to carry out his plans for the slow but effectual suppression of all opposition both at home and abroad.

Armenian war.

The kingdom of Armenia under Tigranes III. was at the height of its power when Clodius, the brother-in-law of Lucullus, then serving under him, was despatched to the royal residence at Tigranocerta to demand the surrender of Mithridates. Tigranes had broken the rival monarchy of Parthia, from which the Greek dynasty of the Seleucides had been previously expelled. He had wrested from it the northern districts of Mesopotamia, and had taken vigorous measures for increasing the wealth of his people by engaging many intelligent Greeks and Syrians in his service. He was the most powerful des pot of the East; his court was attended by a crowd of vassal princes, and four kings, it was said, ran beside his chariot. He had assumed the title of king of kings, borne of old by the despots of Persia, which the Parthian monarch pretended to inherit from them. He had condescended to receive Mithridates as a suppliant, though when in power the king of Pontus had given him scanty support. It was thus that the Romans were enabled to deal with the two greatest powers of Asia separately and in detail. Lucullus could act both with boldness and with caution. In the campaign on which he now entered, vigor and promptitude were essential. The capital of Armenia was well defended by its position among the mountains and the length and severity of its winter season. It was necessary to strike once for all. Lucullus had a small, but well-trained and well-appointed army of veterans. Tigranes surrounded and encumbered himself with a vast cloud of undisciplined barbarians, the flower of whom, consisting 17,000 of mailed cavalry, however formidable in appearance, made but a feeble resistance to the dint of the Roman spear and broadsword. When their ranks were broken they fell back upon the inert masses behind them, and threw them into hopeless confusion. Tigranes made his escape with dastardly precipitation. A bloody massacre ensued, the Romans losing, as was pretended, five men only, while of the enemy 100,000, we are told, were left dead on the field.

In the following year Lucullus advanced his posts still further eastward. He intrigued with the king of Parthia to withdraw him from his alliance with the enemies of the republic, and when he hesitated, threatened to advance into his territories beyond the Tigris. But a spirit of discontent or lassitude had crept over his own soldiers. His lieutenants were dissatisfied with the share of plunder allotted to them the civil officials of the province were disgusted at the equity with which he had curtailed their unrighteous gains. He was constrained to withdraw from the siege of Artaxata, the furthest stronghold of Tigranes, on the banks of the Araxes, and after crowning his victories with a successful assault upon Nisibis, he gave the signal for retreat, leaving the destruction of Mithridates still unaccomplished. Meanwhile the brave proconsul's enemies were making head against him at Rome. The faction of the knights, who demanded all the profits of the civil government in the provinces, had acquired fresh power under the patronage of Pompeius, and from the stain which had been recently cast on their opponents by the misconduct of Verres, prætor of Sicily. The command in the eastern provinces was about to be taken from the victorious *Imperator*, whose only demerit was the spirit with which he had repressed official tyranny, and revived the hopes and happiness of the provincials.

CHAPTER II.
(U.C. 684. B.C. 70.—U.C. 692. B.C. 62.)

Ascendency of Pompeius.—His Subjugation of the Cilician Pirates, and Conquests in the East.

Popularity of Pompeius.

POMPEIUS, on his return from Spain, had accepted the flatteries of the senatorial party, but he had not formally engaged himself to serve it. He preferred to hold all parties in play, and wait upon events. His success against Spartacus confirmed him in the conviction of his own transcendent abilities, and persuaded him that he was necessary to the state, and must one day be invoked as an umpire or dictator to control the administration of affairs. On the restoration of peace he was piqued at the spirit with which a rising public man, C. Julius Cæsar, the nephew of Marius, and heir to a portion of his influence, was attacking the chiefs of the oligarchy for malversation in the provinces. The proceeding was popular, and Pompeius determined to follow in the same track, and seem at least to take the lead in it. He encouraged ahold young orator, M. Tullius Cicero, to denounce the crimes of Verres. Notorious as he was, this culprit was power fully supported. The nobles, conscious of the importance of the case, rallied strenuously around him. His defence was undertaken by Hortensius, the ablest advocate of their party, the favorite of the judges, the "king," as he was called, of the tribunals. Could they get the process postponed to the year ensuing, they might expect favor from the prætor, who would have to select the judges for the trial. Every effort was made to gain this point. The prosecutor was young and in experienced; he was little known, being a "new man," a citizen of the obscure Volscian *municipium* of Arpinum, of an equestrian family indeed, but of no civic distinction at Rome. He had already pleaded with great ability on some former occasions, and had evinced much spirit in resisting the application of a law of Sulla, even during the dictator's lifetime. As quæstor in Sicily, a few years before, he had gained credit for purity as well as for activity. The Sicilians themselves placed the conduct of their impeachment in his hands. He began by a display of judicious firmness in resisting the call for delay; but at the same time he required on his own part some time to collect evidence, and it was only by the most strenuous efforts that he succeeded in furnishing himself with his proofs without allowing the defence the advantage which it demanded. Popular favor at Rome was strong in his behalf, and the consuls Pompeius and Crassus openly avowed their approval. As soon as he opened his case, Hortensius discreetly counselled submission. Verres declined to plead, and withdrew sullenly into exile. But Cicero was not thus satisfied. He published no only the speeches he had delivered, but the further pleadings he had prepared for the full establishment of his charges; and the series of the Verrine Orations still exists as an imperishable record of proconsular misgovernment. They fell, no doubt, upon many willing ears. The consuls, nothing loth, restored to the knights their share in the *judicia*, and thus broke down the great bulwark of oligarchical authority. To give irresponsible decisions in the law courts had been originally the special privilege of the senate; but this function, which had been grievously abused to party purposes, had been directly transferred by C. Gracchus to the knights, had been divided between both orders by the legislators of the next generation, and again confined exclusively to the first by the reactionary policy of Sulla. Catulus and the most patriotic among the nobles assented cordially to the decorous reform of the Aurelian law, though the proudest and blindest of the party still scowled upon it with ill-suppressed indignation.

Purging of the senate by the censors.

The restoration of the tribunate had already wrested from the senate one-half of the political ascendency which Sulla had extorted for them; the admission of the knights to a share in the *judicia* deprived them of what yet remained. But Pompeius was not yet satisfied. In his new-born zeal for the popular interests, he determined to subject the nobles even to personal degradation. Since the time of Sulla no lustrum had been held. The consuls insisted on the appointment of censors. The citizens were duly numbered, their property valued, the personal merits of the members of the senate passed under review. The names of sixty-four of the order were now expunged from the roll and the whole body, august as it was, could not but feel that it was strictly the instrument of the state, and not its master. All the blood of Sulla's massacres had secured for his political work only eight years of existence.

Pompeius was now at the height of his popularity. The people were delighted at the authority which he had acquired, having been exalted to the consulship while still only a knight, and having extorted from his colleague Crassus, the elect of the nobles, the deepest deference and even subservience. The nobles themselves, though exasperated at the superiority he asserted, and jealous of the interest he was making with the popular faction, could not venture to break with him, and still tried every means to attach him to their own side. The consuls, it was said, regarded each other with coldness. A citizen came forward and asserted that he had been ordered by Jupiter, in a dream, to tell them not to lay down their office without being reconciled. Pompeius maintained a haughty reserve, but Crassus deferentially took his hand, exclaiming, "Romans, it is my part to give way to the great Pompeius, whom you have twice honored with a triumph while he was still only a knight." But Pompeius treated the commons with no less reserve and coldness. He withdrew from the popular business of an advocate; he estranged himself from the Forum, and if he ever appeared in public, took care to surround himself with a retinue of clients and flatterers. He carried into the city the manners of the camp or even of a court. This affectation of royal demeanor was designedly adopted. Doubtless, Pompeius, like other Roman generals before him, had conceived the idea of assuming sovereign authority; but his temperament was cold and sluggish, his ambition was of a passive character; he hoped to have greatness thrust upon him, and he saw in the circumstances of the times many indications that the tyranny would surely devolve on the chief who had patience to wait for it. Meanwhile he was on the watch to seize on any opportunity that might present itself for maintaining or even increasing his acknowledged pre-eminence.

Extent of piracy in the Mediterranean.

Such an opportunity was offered by the alarms which were now excited at Rome by the prevalence of piracy in the Mediterranean waters. From east to west the great inland sea was traversed by the fleets of plunderers who had their strongholds and their arsenals in the bays of Cilicia, but who were probably recruited from bands of lawless wanderers on every coast. The civil wars of Rome had deprived many thousands, not only in Italy, but throughout the provinces, of their ordinary means of subsistence. They had engendered, moreover, a general spirit of licentiousness and a greed of plunder and while the continent was kept under some control by the armies of the republic, the sea was left without a police, and had become the common field of enterprise for buccaneers from all quarters. The Cilician pirates, as they came to be denominated, had assumed a certain political consistency. They claimed to transact business with chiefs and potentates. Sertorius had negotiated with them, when he was seeking an asylum beyond the reach of the Roman army. Spartacus had bargained with them for a passage across the straits of Messana. They might give way indeed to the armed flotillas which convoyed the transports of the republic to Greece or Asia; but they attacked single vessels or small squadrons with increasing audacity, murdering or carrying into captivity Roman citizens and even high magistrates, descending upon farms and villas on the coasts of Italy itself, and sweeping off peaceful travellers from the crown of the Appian way. These injuries and indignities, gross as they were, continued to be long endured; for the magnates of the city and of the provinces found their account in them from the abatement they caused in the price of slaves in the markets of Delos, and other centres of that nefarious traffic. But when, by their attacks upon the corn-vessels from Africa and Sicily, the pirates began to threaten the city with scarcity, the voice of the multitude made itself heard. It was determined to strike at the base of the hostile power. Servilius was charged to carry on a regular war against the public foe. His operations were prolonged through three campaigns, in which he besieged and reduced some maritime posts, and pursued his opponents into the mountains, obtaining for his exploits the title of Isauricus and the honor of a triumph. M. Antonius, and after him Metellus, attacked the pirates in their strongholds in Crete; and from this circumstance Metellus acquired the sur name of Creticus. With much labor and by slow degrees the Roman power was established among these obscure fastnesses; but the vessels of the enemy, skilfully handled, for the most part escaped, and found for themselves other retreats still more inaccessible.

The Gabinian law.

The tribes continued to be threatened with famine as before, and they insisted at any price on the thorough subjugation of the importunate foe. For this object they were ready to sacrifice their political jealousies, and to create a power in the state which should be independent of their annual suffrages and of the vicissitudes of party. In the year B.C. 67, the tribune Gabinius proposed that some veteran statesman—some one who had filled the highest office in the republic—should be invested for three years with absolute authority both by sea and land, as far as fifty miles into the interior, over a belt of soil within which lay all the greatest Cities of the Roman dominion throughout the world. For the moment the crafty intriguer withheld the name of the individual whom he would thus raise to irresponsible power; but both the nobles and the people readily understood that he pointed at the great Pompeius. The nobles would have had Gabinius slain; one of his own colleagues, retained in their interest, put his veto on the resolution. Catulus, who was himself popular with the citizens, pointed out the hazard of exposing a personage so precious to the perils of an untried warfare. "Who could replace Pompeius," he exclaimed, "if Pompeius were lost to you." "Yourself!" cried the people, good-humoredly. Catulus desisted from further opposition; the motion was carried; 500 galleys and 120,000 soldiers were voted, and the resources of the state thrown open to the fortunate aspirant. This vote, it has been often said, was the actual commencement of the empire. It was warmly supported by another candidate for greatness, the heir eventually of more than the power of Pompeius, the future dictator and emperor, C. Julius Cæsar.

Success of Pompeius against the Cilician pirates.
B.C. 67.

As soon as this decree was announced the pirates knew that they would be dealt with in earnest, and withdrew promptly from the coasts of Italy. Stores of grain flowed in, and its price in the Roman market fell at once. The people believed that the mere name of their favorite had finished the war. But Pompeius knew that it was not so, and he had no wish that it should be so. He had obtained imperial powers, and he was determined to make use of them. He chose for his lieutenants twenty-four senators, all men of distinction and experience in command; he divided the Mediterranean into thirteen regions, and appointed a squadron to each. In the space of forty days he had swept the whole western tract of the great inland sea, and driven the enemy into the opposite quarter. The pirates, finding his measures irresistible, made no head against them. Their leaders readily betrayed one another, and the politic commander employed the services of each in the general pursuit. The few that still held out were driven into the creeks and bays of the Cilician coast, where they were defended by their stockades and fortresses; but these, 120 in number, were speedily surrounded and overthrown. Pompeius burnt as many as 1,300 of their vessels, and destroyed all the hostile magazines and arsenals. His captives he lodged at various spots along the shores where they had previously carried desolation. Ninety days sufficed to terminate the contest. The success was certainly complete for the time; but piracy was too easy and tempting a trade to be permanently eradicated. Whenever, during the civil troubles which succeeded, Rome allowed herself to neglect the police of the seas, the coasts of the eastern Mediterranean again swarmed with maritime robbers; and the Levant has continued to this day to be similarly infested under similar circumstances. But the Roman people had no misgivings. They rejoiced in the plenty which seemed to be now assured to them; they exulted in the success of their admired hero, and not only lavished upon him caresses and honors, but allowed him to insult the other chiefs of the state, and trample upon the officers who ventured to exercise the authority entrusted to them. He required the distinguished consular Q. Metellus, who had obtained an independent command for the reduction of the Cretan brigands before his own extraordinary appointment, to desist from his operations, and when Metellus demurred to the order, actually sent one of his lieutenants to assist the enemy whom he was employed in subduing. The people pardoned the affront to their own majesty; but history has not failed to record the vexation even of the great commander's friends at the jealousy he evinced, in this and many other instances, of all who seemed in any degree to trench upon his own exclusive pretensions.

Investment of Pompeius with supreme command in the East.

Meanwhile the opposition of the *publicani*, the greedy collectors of the taxes in Asia, and of their supporters in the city, had reduced Lucullus to enforced investment of inactivity. Some of his troops had been withdrawn from his standard, and transferred to Glabrio in Bithynia; another portion had been put under the command of Marcius Rex in Cilicia. Mithridates and Tigranes had seized the opportunity for attack. Legions and detachments had suffered severe defeats, which Lucullus, with weakened forces, had with difficulty repaired. His own mutinous soldiers had refused to be led in pursuit of the enemy; and once more the allied kings had invaded the Roman provinces, and driven the new commanders of the legions far back towards the Ægean. But Pompeius was now at hand on the coast of Cilicia. The intrigues of his partizans at home had fully ripened. The tribune Manilius stepped forward and argued that the conqueror of the pirates should be at once charged with the conquest of the arch-enemy Mithridates, who had baffled for twenty years the greatest captains of the republic. To accomplish so great a service he must be invested with sovereign power over all the East. The authority he already wielded against the pirates must be extended and enlarged. Here was another step towards empire, but it seemed a small step. Necessity knew no law. Many forces from many quarters combined to support the proposition. The nobles were alarmed and reluctant; but the Marian party were all the more urgent for its adoption, and the Marians were now led by a strong and able Chief in the person of Cæsar. Crassus himself was well inclined to encourage any motion which tended to establish a precedent for unlimited authority. Cicero was carried away partly by his genuine enthusiasm in favor of abler and stronger men than himself, partly, no doubt, by the flatteries lavished upon him by Pompeius, by Crassus, and by Cæsar, who all felt that his eloquence might be of use to them, while the nobles continued to repel him as an upstart unworthy of their favor or countenance. The lofty spirit of Catulus was of no avail against so many and such various forces. The bill of Manilius was carried in the tribes with enthusiasm, and the sullen opposition of the senate was almost contemptuously overruled.

Effects of Roman ascendancy in the East.

The Romans ascribed to Pompeius the character of a profound dissembler. They said that on this elevation of fortune he pretended to be deeply troubled, and professed to regret the honors which were thrust upon him. But his acts evinced no abatement of pride or resolution. He assumed at once all the powers that were entrusted to him, and chose his lieutenants and appointed them to their respective services with alacrity. As soon as he had collected his troops around him, he summoned the allies and dependents of the republic in the East to attend upon him and take orders from his camp, while, at the same time, he seemed studiously to humiliate his predecessor in command, by traversing his orders and political arrangements. The two generals met, the one advancing, the other retiring, in Galatia. Pompeius insulted Lucullus with pretended compliments and actual affronts; but Lucullus took care to inform his countrymen that he had himself already broken the power of the enemy whom his rival was sent to crush, and that the final overthrow of Mithridates was already prepared to his successor's hands, as had been the overthrow of Spartacus and of Sertorius. Pompeius, however, did not intend to confine his views to the destruction of any single enemy. His commission extended to the complete settlement of the affairs of the East. The kingdoms of Armenia and Parthia were to be rendered subservient to the policy of Rome. The alliance between Tigranes and Phraates was to be finally broken, and these princes were to be made mutually jealous of one another and severally dependent upon the support of the republic. The frontier of the Euphrates was to be secured by placing its bridges in the hands of lesser vassals, who could at any convenient moment be transformed into subjects. The eastern shores of the Mediterranean were to be reduced to the condition of Roman provinces. Pompeius finally annexed the rich and populous realm of Syria, and found an opportunity to interfere in the disputes of the reigning family in Judæa, and establish a dependent sovereign on the throne of Jerusalem. The mingled craft and violence with which he acted throughout these transactions are sufficiently disgusting; but it must be confessed that no portion of human annals is more odious than the history of the tyrants of Judæa who had risen on the fall of the Syrian power in that country. Every step, however harsh and oppressive, that Rome took, in displacing the native rule and preparing the way for her own, served to mitigate some of the sufferings of the people, and to pacify at least their internal discords.

Overthrow and death of Mithridates. B.C. 63.

While engaged in these operations, and setting up or putting down at pleasure thrones and dynasties, Pompeius regarded himself as the autocrat of the East, the king of kings, another Xerxes. He had wrested from Mithridates the kingdom of Pontus, and pursued him along the coast of the Euxine beyond the Phasis; but from thence he had turned to the east and to the south, and had allowed his baffled and dispirited adversary to maintain himself in the Cimmerian Chersonese, on the furthest confines of his possessions. He was content to foster intrigues against him in his own family, and it was by the defection of his favorite son Pharnaces that the king was prevented from executing an audacious plan of at tacking Italy herself on the side of Thrace and Illyria. Pharnaces entered into relations with the Romans. Mithridates marched against him, but was at last abandoned by his own soldiers, and was reduced, it was said, in his extremity to take poison. The popular account affirmed that his system had been so fortified by the habitual use of antidotes that the poison took no effect, but this is one of the marvellous stories of antiquity to which modern science will hardly allow us to give credit. At all events, the terrible Mithridates fell at last upon the sword of one of his own Gaulish captives.

Extent of Roman supremacy in the East.

Pompeius was himself in Judæa when the death of his chief adversary was announced to him. He was now at leisure to advance northward and secure the fruits of this crowning success. At Amisus in Pontus he received from Pharnaces the dead body of Mithridates, to make him doubly sure of his triumph, and policy rather than generosity induced him to give it royal obsequies at Sinope, and thus render the fact of his death notorious throughout the regions in which the mere name of the great tyrant had sufficed to raise innumerable armies. The success of Pompeius was now complete, but it had been gained from the first over exhausted or distracted enemies. He had obtained vast advantages for the republic, yet he could hardly be said to have reaped fresh laurels for himself. But his reputation as a captain was already well established, and Rome was content to ascribe the extension of her empire in the East to a military genius which, in fact, he had hardly exercised at all. She had embraced within her frontiers a number of dependent sovereigns. Deiotarus occupied the vassal throne of Galatia; Attalus affected to reign in Paphlagonia; Ariobarzanes in Cappadocia; but Pontus, Cilicia, and Syria were definitively added to the list of the provinces. Beyond the lines of her stations and garrisons the republic supported the sovereignty of Pharnaces on the Bosporus, and of Herod in Palestine, and she completely detached the kingdom of Armenia from the influence of Parthia. In the course of time a great portion of these regions became absorbed in the empire; but it was only occasionally, and but for a brief period, that the outposts of the Roman power were pushed beyond the eastern limits at which Pompeius had placed them. The senate vaunted the patriotic services of the Imperator, to whom it still looked for the maintenance of its own ascendency. It trusted, though not without some misgiving, that the camps in Asia had given it a second Sulla to assert the prerogatives of the oligarchy. The dissensions in the city were threatening it with a revival of the claims of the Marians, but it still clung with fitful hope to its powerful army and its victorious general.

C. Julius Cæsar.

Pompeius had seemed indeed to break with the Optimates when he allowed the tribunes to raise the people in his interest, and thrust upon him the vast and irregular powers of the Gabinian and the Manilian laws. But they could hardly deny that the first of these was a measure of pressing necessity, and that they had themselves given occasion to the second by the abandonment of their ill-used champion Lucullus. They now expected, doubt less, that the altered state of affairs at Rome would compel the chief of the army to make common cause with them for his own sake; for the course of events had raised up a rival there of whom he could not fail to be jealous. The young C. Julius Cæsar had become a power in the state. Descended from an ancient patrician race, which claimed as its eponym, Julus, the son of Æneas, the grandson of Anchises and the goddess Venus, he could point to the images of many noble ancestors, though none of them had attained the highest distinction in the Roman annals. Cæsar's birth and origin might thus have attached him to the party of the senate and the Optimates, which comprised the chief historical houses of the commonwealth, but Marius, as it chanced, had married his aunt, and his early predilections were thus engaged to the Marians; his first marriage, also, which he had contracted as a mere boy, was with a daughter of Cinna. As a youth, however, he gave no special token of devotion to a cause or aptitude for public affairs. He plunged from the first into a career of dissipation, redeemed only by the elegance of his tastes and manners; but be early embarrassed himself with a load of debt, while he made himself many personal enemies by the looseness of his amatory intrigues. No matron, it was said, could resist his beauty; while his gracious manners exercised a wondrous fascination over the gravest statesman. Sulla, indeed, had divined his genius, and warned some who had spoken slightingly of him, that in the young Cæsar there was many a Marius. But Pompeius, who had come in contact with him on his return from Spain, in the height of his own ascendency, had deemed him no more than a serviceable dependent; and Cicero, when he looked around him for a party to serve and a patron to follow, had persuaded himself that the state had nothing to fear, and he had himself nothing to gain, from the elegant debauchee who trailed his gown so loosely in the Forum. Cæsar, however, was conscious of his own powers; nor did he place less reliance on his own fortune. It is related that in his youth he fell into the hands of the pirates on the coast of Asia, and when they offered to release him for a ransom of twenty talents, insisted on their taking no less than fifty, assuring them at the same time that he would have them all hanged at last—a threat which he soon found means of actually carrying into effect. He was still a private student at Rhodes, holding no military appointment, when hearing that Mithridates was attacking some allies of the republic, he collected troops on his own account, and levied successful wars against the most redoubtable of its enemies.

Motions of the tribune Cornelius.

During the years that followed, Cæsar continued to watch the career of Pompeius, and meditated rivalling him in the favor of the citizens. But his first care was to support the measures, such as those of Gabinius and Manilius, which were brought forward by the great man's creatures for enhancing his personal ascendency. Such measures served Cæsar's designs in two ways; they rendered men's minds more and more familiar with the notion of autocratic government, to which all classes seemed to look as the inevitable issue of affairs, and at the same time they helped to increase the jealousy of the nobles towards the man who had once been their minister, but who was now making himself more and more independent of them. Cæsar beheld with satisfaction the motions of the tribune Cornelius, for curbing the excessive usury which the nobles had allowed themselves to exact for the loans negotiated with them by the provinces. The tribune was encountered by furious opposition, and opposition was overcome by violence in the comitia. When an impeachment was hurled against the obnoxious officer who, it seems, had not scrupled to disregard the veto of a colleague whose services had been purchased by the senate, a tumult ensued. Manilius ventured to defend the culprit, and tried to overawe his opponents with the name of Pompeius. The consuls, however, had the courage to exert military force, and the affair was subjected to legal process. Cicero, at the instigation of Pompeius, or of his adherents, was retained to defend the accused, and ventured to plead the favor in which he was held by the redoubted champion of the republic, who was engaged far away in its defence and aggrandizement. The arguments of the orator proved successful. The charge was allowed to drop. The countenance thus given to popular violence was of fatal significance. From that time it was again and again repeated with aggravated fury. The senate and the people were thus committed to a struggle which could not fail to demand the interference of a power paramount to both. It required little foresight to anticipate the effect of the conqueror's triumphant return from the East, unless indeed his threatened supremacy should be counterbalanced by the creation of a rival power supported by an overwhelming popular feeling at home. It was to the creation of such a power that Cæsar was directing all his resources.

Cæsar's ædileship.

In the year 65 Cæsar obtained the ædileship in conjunction with Bibulus, the candidate of the nobles. This office was charged with providing amusements for the populace. It required an enormous outlay of money, but it opened the way, through the favor of the people, to the highest public honors. Cæsar played his game boldly. He charmed the populace by the expenses he lavishly incurred, and especially by the profusion of silver bullion with which he decorated the furniture and implements of the arena. Plunged already deep in debt, he continued to borrow on the credit of his genius and his rising fortunes. If the wealthy Bibulus equalled Cæsar in munificence, the people gave him no credit for generosity; nor were the manners of the penniless adventurer less ingratiating than his reckless prodigality. Bibulus was fain to liken himself to Pollux, who, though he possessed a temple in conjunction with his twin brother, heard it always called by the name of Castor rather than by his own. Cæsar could now rely on the clamorous support of the populace for the bold measures on which he ventured. He had already irritated the nobles by parading the proscribed bust of Marius in public; he now erected the statue of their fallen enemy among the ornaments of the Capitol, and surrounded it with the trophies of his victories. The people shouted with delight; the nobles scowled indignantly. Catulus determined to bring him to punishment for a violation of the law of attainder. Catulus was not only the chief leader of the senate and the political heir of Sulla, he was the son of the noblest victim of the Marian massacres. He accused Cæsar of ulterior designs; he declared that he was now assaulting the republic, not covertly with mines, but with the battering-ram openly. Cæsar defended himself in the senate house, and even there he succeeded in foiling his accuser; but he extorted his acquittal from the fears of the assembly rather than from its justice or its favor. The nobles contented themselves with a prompt retaliation. When about to resign the ædileship Cæsar demanded a public mission to take possession of Egypt, in virtue of the will of the king Ptolemæus Alexander. This country, through which the commerce of the East passed into Europe, was regarded as the wealthiest in the world. It offered a magnificent prey to the rapacious republic, and an ample harvest to the fortunate officer who should be appointed to annex it. Crassus and Cæsar disputed this rich booty, but the senate evaded the demands of both equally. A tribune named Papius was engaged to demand that all foreigners, and especially Cæsar's clients, the transpadane Gauls, should be removed from the city; and when his most vehement partisans were thus disabled, Cæsar probably himself assisted in preventing the success of his rival. The government allowed the bequest of the Egyptian monarch, whether real or pretended, to remain in abeyance, rather than subject itself to the peril of flinging so splendid a prize into the hands of any one of the citizens.

Cæsar impeaches Rabirius.
U.C. 690. B.C. 65.

But Cæsar obtained a seat on the tribunal which inquired into cases of murder. This appointment had a political significance which he could turn to account. Hitherto he had done no more than protest by silent tokens against the dictatorship of Sulla; he now resolved to brand it with a legal stigma. He cited before him and condemned as political offenders two men who had acted as Sulla's instruments of blood. He went still further back in his inquisition—he induced one of the tribunes to accuse an aged senator, Rabirius, of the slaughter of the traitor Saturninus. Both Cicero and Hortensius were engaged by the nobles to defend the victim; but the people seemed to exult in the audacious injustice of the process; for it was well known, first, that Rabirius had not done the deed; secondly, that the real slayer had been publicly justified at the time; and, lastly, that the transaction had occurred as much as thirty-six years before, and might well deserve to be buried in oblivion after so many political revolutions. The appeal of Rabirius would actually have been rejected but for the adroitness of the prætor. Metellus Celer, who suddenly struck the flag which waved from the Janiculum during the public assembly of the tribes. In ancient times the striking of this flag was the signal that the Etruscans were advancing to attack the city. Instantly all business was suspended, the comitia were dissolved, and the citizens rushed sword in hand to man the walls. The formality still held its ground among a people singularly tenacious of traditional usages; and now again the multitude, which had just clamored for innocent blood, laughed at the trick by which its fury was baffled, and acquiesced in the suspension of the proceedings. Cæsar had gained his point in alarming and mortifying the senate, and allowed the matter to drop, which he had never perhaps intended to push to extremity.

Cæsar chief pontiff. B.C. 63.

Labienus, the tribune who had been Cæsar's agent in this matter, procured his patron a further gratification, in requiring the abrogation of the Cornelian law, by which Sulla had withdrawn from the people the nomination to the college of pontiffs. The chief place in that body was now vacant, and the popular election promptly fell upon the new favorite, who was placed thereby in command of a great political engine, and whose person was rendered legally inviolable. Neither the notorious laxity of his moral principles, nor his avowed contempt for the religious traditions of the multitude, hindered Cæsar's advancement to the highest office of the national worship. It sufficed that he should perform the stated functions of his post, and maintain the prescriptive usages on which the state pretended to repose her safety and well-being. Cæsar's triumph was the more complete as it was gained over Catulus, who had contemptuously offered to buy off his opposition by a loan of money. But Cæsar had declared that he would borrow more and more largely from any quarter, rather than forego a prize which had become indeed necessary for his personal security. He was menaced with an impeachment for treason against the state, and, whether he was conscious of guilt or not, his enemies, he knew, were not more scrupulous than himself. When the hour of election arrived he said to his mother, on quitting his house, "This day your son will be either chief pontiff or an exile."

CHAPTER III.
(U.C. 691. B.C. 63.—U.C. 694. B.C. 60.)

STATE OF PARTIES IN THE CITY.—CONSULSHIP OF CICERO, AND CONSPIRACY OF CATILINA.

Leaders of the Nobles.

THE nobles might begin already to feel insecure, and while they still clung to the hope that Pompeius would protect them against their adversaries at home, they were anxious to provide for their own defence, without relying on his precarious assistance. On the whole, they were content, perhaps, that he should continue absent from the city, while he removed the legions with him to a distance, and left them to depend on the civil arm and the irregular support of their own clients and dependents. Africa had been wrested from the rival faction of the Marians; Gaul and Spain had been placed under the government of their own partisans. The cohorts which watched over Italy and the city itself were for the most part officered by captains of their own choice, and the veterans of Sulla, scattered throughout the peninsula on lands assigned them by the dictator, secured them, it might be thought, an ample reserve both of influence and of military power. But the party of the optimates wanted leaders. The chief men among them, however eminent from birth, wealth, and personal distinction, were uniformly deficient both in the power of attracting adherents and also of commanding them. Catulus, the most high-minded and honorable of all, wanted spirit, decision, and force of character, as he had too plainly shown in his contest with Lepidus. Lucullus, partly from indolence and self-indulgence, partly no doubt from mortification at the treatment he had received from his own party, no longer cared to mingle actively in state affairs. The policy of Crassus was simply selfish; he was seeking, or rather, in accordance with his sluggish nature, was waiting for ascendency over all parties, and was justly distrusted by all. Silanus,

Murena, and others were not incompetent indeed to discharge the high office which became their eminence in rank and civil experience, but were plainly unequal to the task of leading and controlling. Hortensius possessed much influence as an orator, but his position hardly entitled him to command a political party; and generally the possessors of the greatest wealth among a wealthy nobility were more addicted to the enjoyment of personal luxuries than to the conduct of public affairs. The most active and vigorous of their class was not one of the wealthiest or the noblest. The authority which M. Porcius Cato eventually exercised among them was gained by his own actual merits and exertions; but he, too, with all his zeal and energy, was lacking in discretion and judgment, and promised to offer only violent and intemperate counsels at a crisis which demanded the utmost moderation and circumspection.

M. Porcius Cato.

Cato inherited the name, the temper, and the principles of the illustrious censor his great-grandfather, and therewith enjoyed in no slight degree the respect and confidence of the Roman people. He believed, as devoutly as his ancestor, in the mission of a superior caste of citizens to rule the state; in the right of the Roman people, the lords of the human race, to hold the world in bondage; in the absolute authority of the husband over the wife, the parent over the child, the master over his bondman. His temper, indeed, was more kindly than his principles, and the gleams of good humor which break occasionally through the cloud of prejudices in which he studiously involved himself, afford some relief to the general harshness of his character and conduct. Born in the year 95 B.C., he had witnessed the close of the Social war, and resented, as a child, the compromise in which that struggle resulted. Nevertheless, his feelings had revolted from the bloody measures with which Sulla had avenged it, and he alone of his party had sighed over their most signal victories, and lamented the cruel retaliation they had demanded. From early life he had trained himself in all the hardness of the ancient manners which had become now generally obsolete. Inured to frugality and of simple tastes, he had resisted all temptation to rapine and extortion. Enrolling himself in the priesthood of Apollo, he acknowledged perhaps a divine call to a higher life in the practice of bodily self-denial. He imbibed the doctrines of the Stoic philosophy, the rigidity of which accorded well with his own temper, and he strove under their guidance to direct his public conduct by the strictest rules of private integrity. If he failed, it was through the infirmity of our common nature, not from personal vanity or caprice; but it cannot be denied that the exigencies of public affairs drove him, as well as others, to many a sordid compromise with his noble principles. The strength to which he aspired became, indeed, the source of manifold weakness. It made him vain of his superior virtues, confident in his judgments, morose and ungenerous, a blind observer of forms, and impracticable in his prejudices. A party composed of such men as Cato would have been ill-matched with the ranks of pliant intriguers opposed to them on every side; but when the selfish, indolent, and unprincipled chose themselves a champion of a character so alien from their own, there could be no hearty and, therefore, no fruitful alliance between the leader and his followers.

M. Tullius Cicero.

As yet, however, the ascendency of Cato in the councils of the optimates was unconfirmed. The senate hoped to secure in the rising orator, Cicero, a supporter whom they might first use for their own purposes, and then, if convenient, cast away. For M. Tullius Cicero, the son of a Volscian knight, with neither birth, nor connection, nor wealth, might be easily induced, as they supposed, to serve them with his undoubted talents for the sake of the distinctions to which they could introduce him, and might not be too exacting in the devotion he would expect from them in return. Cicero had sought at the commencement of his career to attach himself to Pompeius; but Pompeius had always treated him, as he treated others, with coldness, and the great captain was, moreover, absent. Again, Cicero had admired Cæsar, and inclined to lean upon his support; but the dangerous policy of Cæsar had become lately developed, and it was plain that the aspirant's choice must now be made between the senate and the champion of the people. Public men, indeed, were now well aware that the state was in danger from the machinations of a revolutionary cabal which were swiftly ripening to an explosion. The real designs of the infamous Catilina and his associates must indeed always remain shrouded in mystery. The accounts we have received of them come from the mouths of their opponents exclusively. The declamations of Cicero, supported in the main by the sententious history of Sallust, became the recognised text on which the later Roman writers relied, and beyond these there exist no contemporary materials for forming a judgment upon the facts. Doubtless, it was the interest of the nobles to blacken the character of the conspirators to the utmost. Nevertheless, it is impossible to deny, and on the whole it would be unreasonable to doubt, that such a conspiracy there really was, and that the very existence of the commonwealth was for a moment seriously imperilled.

Conspiracy of Catilina.

The civil wars had left society at Rome in a state of general disturbance. The license of the times had engendered a reckless spirit of selfishness and violence. Criminal ambitions had been fostered by the spectacle of successful treacheries. The highest honors had fallen to the most worthless of men, who had had the audacity to strike for them. At the same time the plunder of the East had flooded Rome with wealth and luxuries. It had created a class of men who did not scruple to employ their riches in the purchase of venal votes, and the dignity of the common wealth had been too commonly prostituted to vulgar arrogance. Money had been easily made, but it had been no less easily lost. Even in the highest orders if many had become suddenly rich, more, no doubt, had found themselves no less suddenly impoverished. The state lay in danger from the intrigues of the one class, still more perhaps from the violence of the other. A cry rose more and more loud among the young reprobates who hung on the skirts of the aristocracy for relief from their debts, for wiping out the accounts against them, if necessary, in blood. Such men were led by accomplished bravoes, such as L. Sergius Catilina, notorious himself as a ruined spendthrift, and distinguished at the same time for his personal bravery as well as by his high connections. The city was rife with stories of this man's wild and wicked deeds. He had cruelly murdered an enemy of the dictator; he had assassinated his own brother; he had sacrificed his youthful son with a view to a union with a rich but profligate woman. Yet with the stigma of a broken fortune and of all these crimes upon him, we are required to believe that Catilina had advanced far in the career of public favor and of civil honors, and had at last proposed himself as a candidate for the consulship. Nay, more, the discreet and decorous Cicero had not hesitated to join with him in competition for the office, and had undertaken his defence against a charge of malversation in the province which he had been already allowed to administer. Even now he was commonly believed to be engaged in a plot against the state, and a vague rumor pointed even to men so distinguished as Crassus and Cæsar as associated with him.

Cicero becomes consul.
U.C. 691. B.C. 63.

The nobles had little confidence in any of their natural leaders, and when the ascendency of their party, if not the actual safety of the state, was threatened by a plot which they were perhaps unable to unmask, they were willing to condone Cicero's offence in the impeachment of Verres, and the court he had assiduously paid to the people, while they lent their influence to raise him to the consulship. They managed at the same time to associate with him one of their own order, named Antonius, who, it seems, was but a faithless partisan after all. Cicero was naturally elated at the elevation he had attained, and easily believed himself necessary to the party which had thus sought his assistance. He now devoted himself to the interests of the senate, drew more and more away from the adherents of Pompeius, from Crassus, and from Cæsar; and when the leader of the people proposed an agrarian law through the tribune Rullus, he denounced and overruled the attempt. The public domain in Italy had been almost wholly alienated from the state. The veterans of Sulla had been recompensed with grants of all the land which was available for the enrichment of the poorer citizens; but the conquests of the republic in Gaul and Spain had supplied a large reserve of territory, and Rullus had proposed that by the sale of this reserved land funds should be raised for the endowment of the lower populace. It might be expected that the loss thence resulting to the revenue would be amply balanced by the tribute which was flowing more and more largely from the East. The motion seems to have been generally politic; but it may be presumed that it was with party views that Cæsar had urged, and it was with such views undoubtedly that Cicero and the senate had opposed it. The contest served to bind the aspiring consul and his new friends more closely together.

Preparations of the conspirators.

Meanwhile, the intrigues of Catilina were ripening, and Cicero was keenly watching them, and gathering into his hand the clues which should lead to their exposure. It seems that the arch-conspirator, while selecting his associates and preparing his resources even for civil war, if necessary, was still bent on obtaining the consulship for which he offered himself a second time and while he still retained a hope of success in this critical undertaking, he studiously refrained from committing himself to open violence. Cicero, however, had decided that it was better for his party, better for the state, to meet Catilina as an avowed traitor than to allow him to attain the legitimate power of the highest magistracy. He applied himself to the support of Silanus and Murena, both of them, as has been said, chiefs among the optimates, but both of them held in regard by Crassus and Cæsar, and fitted accordingly to secure the suffrage of all the party leaders. It was only by outrageous bribery that Catilina could hope to succeed against such a combination; and here, too, Cicero contrived to baffle him by promising a decree of ten years' banishment against the candidate who should be convicted of buying the votes of the people. This decisive measure drove the conspirator to despair. His preparations for the alternative on which he had resolved were already far advanced; arms had been collected; the restless veterans of Sulla had been tampered with, and abundant aid elsewhere secured. It was said that the fleet at Ostia, which commanded the access of the corn vessels to the city, had been gained. The officers in command in Africa, and even in Spain, had promised assistance. The garrisons of these neighboring provinces might be waited to Italy before the first news of disturbance could reach the faithful legions of the East. Even the loyalty of the consul Antonius was at the best doubtful; but Cicero would not allow it to be called in question. The band of traitors certainly comprised, however, various personages of distinction and influence. Sallust has recorded the names of several senators and as many knights. Cornelius Lentulus was designated prætor for the ensuing year, a vain and ambitious off in their arms, and among them was C. Scribonius Curio, who afterwards played a notable part in his public career.

Their execution.

The consul had thus armed himself with sufficient powers. He allowed of not a moment's delay, but went himself to the house where Lentulus was detained on the Palatine, and led him with his own hand to the Tullianum, the prison under the Capitoline. The other culprits were brought to the same spot by the magistrates who had them in custody. The executioners were at hand. Lentulus was strangled first, and Cathegus, Gabinius, Statilius, and Ceparius, all men of eminence, suffered successively. The consul attended to the last, and as he traversed the Forum on his way homeward, he muttered to the crowd who were anxiously looking for him, "They have lived." The people accepted the intimation of their fate without applause, but also without a murmur.

Defeat and death of Catilina, early in U.C. 692. B.C.62.

The state was saved by this prompt execution, but the treason still survived. Catilina himself was at large, and his occult conspiracy had burst forth into open rebellion. The crisis was still a grave one; but Cicero had calculated the risk beforehand, and was confident of his power to control it. He had associated the senate in a deed of blood which could only be justified by success; and at the same time, by proving to them the power which they could really wield, and the strength of their position if they would act up to it, he had encouraged them to defy the factions of the city, and to regard even the great Pompeius himself as their minister and not their master. The patron they suspected and feared had withdrawn, he might say, from the city, and left them exposed to the evil designs of the Marians, and to every other criminal ambition; but trusting in themselves alone they had exposed the machinations of their enemies, slain many of their leaders, and driven the remnant to make their last stand in a position in which they could be easily exterminated. The presence of their hasty levies had already put down the movements of insurrection throughout the greater part of Italy. In Etruria alone the resistance was still obstinate. Cicero, however, had purchased the co-operation of his colleague Antonius by ceding to him the province of Macedonia; and while this vacillating leader was allowed to hold the ostensible command of the troops in front of Catilina, he was placed actually under the control of more trusty lieutenants, Sextius and Petreius. At the same time Metellus Creticus, a loyal officer, operated in the enemies' rear, cut off his recruits from the Cisalpine, and was ready to intercept his retreat. Catilina had collected 20,000 men, but they were imperfectly equipped and disciplined. He despaired of success in arms, but he exerted all his artifices to win over the chiefs of the armies opposed to him. But delay was fatal. The bulk of his levies deserted him. Antonius might feign sickness to excuse his own want of activity; but his place was supplied by more determined opponents, and Catilina, reduced to extremity, could only fling himself desperately upon their hostile array, and sell dearly his own life and the lives of his few devoted adherents. His body was found in advance of his own lines among a heap of slaughtered enemies. His head was sent to Rome to assure the senate of their triumph, and the issue of the battle of Pistoria raised their spirits to a pitch of intoxication. They were now prepared to defy Pompeius; Cæsar and Crassus they despised; they had made good use of the talents of the upstart Cicero, and henceforth they could afford to throw him away whenever it should appear expedient to do so.

Cicero in controversy with Cato.

The conspirators had been put to death on December 5, B.C. 63, as the calendar then stood. The defeat and slaughter of Catilina did not take place till March, B.C.62. In the interval Silanus and Murena had taken their seats as consuls. Sulpicius, the great jurist of the republic, had been defeated at the election in the previous summer, and had accused his successful opponents of bribery. Cicero had exerted himself to stifle a struggle between men who were all adherents of the same party in the state; but Cato had resented the misconduct of the consuls designate, and had supported with vehemence and pertinacity the suit of the defeated candidate. Cicero undertook the defence in person; nevertheless, he refrained with great tact from embittering the untoward dispute, and confined himself to good-humored banter of the impracticable principles of the Stoic philosopher, raising a laugh against him, which Cato himself, with equal good humor, retorted. "See what a witty consul we have!" was the only remark he made upon it; nor did he harbor any feeling of displeasure against the orator who both ridiculed and defeated him.

Intrigues and disturbances in the city, U.C. 692. B.C. 62.

Cæsar had already obtained the prætorship in the elections for the year 62. Pompeius, with his eye still on the city, had sent his creature, Metellus Nepos, to secure one seat at least in his interest on the bench of tribunes. Cato was in the act of withdrawing in disgust from the city, when he met the agent of the ambitious pro-consul on his route to the scene of election, and determined himself to return for the purpose of thwarting his manœuvres. He presented himself to the tribes at the comitia, and obtained a place among the tribunes along with the opponent whom he had set himself to watch and baffle. But the nobles had greater cause of alarm from the rising estimation of Cæsar, whom the people were taking more especially into favor. After the daring act by which Lentulus and his associates had been so summarily punished, they trembled for the safety of one whom the nobles had chosen to suspect of complicity in their plot. On one occasion when he happened to be detained longer than usual in the senate house, they surrounded the place and tumultuously demanded to be reassured by his actual appearance. Cæsar was nothing daunted. He continued to vex and harass the leaders of the optimates. Catulus had been appointed, as the most eminent of the ruling party in the state, to carry out the restoration of the Capitol after the conflagration under Sulla. He might now expect that his name should be honorably commemorated on the front of the new edifice. But Cæsar audaciously interposed with a charge of malversation, and urged the people to demand that the honor of the auspicious work should be transferred to Pompeius. This was, perhaps, a mere bravado. The nobles, by great exertion, succeeded in warding off the blow, and the name of Catulus was duly inscribed on the great national monument. But they were not only irritated by the affront; they were alarmed at the design which lurked too plainly behind it. Metellus Nepos, in the interest of his patron, connected himself with Cæsar and the sacrifices. His turn had come to take the command of a prætorial province, and the Further Spain had fallen to him; but he lacked means to make the necessary outlay. He had already borrowed, as we have seen, of his friends and partizans, and wanted, as he carelessly said, a sum of 2,000,000*l.* sterling to be "worth nothing." The purse of Crassus was now his last resource, and this purse Crassus was content to open to him for the sake of the connection it offered him with one whom he regarded as a bold but an obsequious dependent.

Clodius profanes the mysteries of the Bona Dea.
U.C. 693. B.C. 61

Nor was this the only way in which fortune smiled on Cæsar's aspirations. At the moment when the violent action of the senate against him had attached his own party more closely to his side, an incident had occurred which threatened to create a schism between them. P. Clodius, a dissolute youth and a favorite with the people, had introduced himself into Cæsar's house in female attire, during the celebration of the rites of the Bona Dea, from which all males were rigorously excluded. Discovered by the outcry of a servant-maid who had recognised him, he was hastily expelled; but the affair, which originated probably in private intrigue, became known and denounced by interested parties as a grave public scandal. The senate affected alarm; the pontiffs were consulted; Cæsar's wife, Pompeia, seemed to be an accomplice in the crime. A solemn inquiry was instituted, and Cæsar was expected to prosecute the offender, who was a friend of his own, as well as a favorite with the popular party. The senate passed a decree that he should not quit Rome for his province till an affair which thus compromised his interests had been brought to a conclusion. Cæsar sacrificed his wife to save his party connections. He divorced Pompeia, not, as he said, because he judged her guilty, but because, as he proudly proclaimed, "the wife of Cæsar should be above suspicion." The phrase had immense success. The populace were charmed at its high-flown magnanimity. The nobles themselves smiled—possibly at its ingenuity. Clodius succeeded in gaining the suffrages of his judges by favor and bribery; Crassus lent the money, but Cæsar was reputed to have negotiated the loan.

Policy of Pompeius on his return to Rome. U.C. 692. B.C. 62.—Triumph of Pompeius. U.C. 693. B.C. 61.

The restless adversary of the nobles hastened to quit the city for his province, well satisfied at having thrown into it the seeds of discord, which would keep the commonwealth from subsiding into a state of settled government until his return. The venture was indeed a bold one, but Cæsar's calculations proved to be well founded. Pompeius had but just returned from the East, with a numerous army. He had only to show himself at the gates of the city at the head of his legions, and it would be impossible to resist whatever demands he might choose to advance. He might require the honor of a triumph; he might insist on the recognition by the state of the acts of his long-protracted government; jealous as the senate was of its authority, and well disposed to thwart and affront him, it could not dare to withhold such marks of approbation. But Pompeius was supposed to have further objects in view. He might regard himself as the heir of Sulla, and claim the dictatorship. He might emulate the oriental potentates with whom he had so long been associated, whose manners and principles he had studied; he might aspire to the diadem. The times indeed were hardly ripe for such a concession; but the most desperate resistance would have been for the moment unavailing. The master of the legions was really the master of the commonwealth. But Cæsar had studied the character of the great commander, and had taken his measure accurately. Pompeius had not the spirit, nor had he the genius of a usurper. It would be too much to say of him that he was withheld from violence by constitutional and patriotic principles. He had never refused the honors or the powers, however excessive, that had been thrust into his hands. He had never shown abhorrence from the shedding of Roman blood, or from other acts of violence, when backed by authority legally committed to him. But his temper was naturally sluggish, and lacked the ardor of a youthful ambition. His advance had been too early and too rapid, and everything had hitherto yielded to him too easily, to allow him to doubt that the same fortune would follow him to the end. He was imbued with a calm conviction that "if fate would have him king, fate would crown him," and that no effort was required on his part to pluck the fruit which was ready to drop into his lap of its own accord. Accordingly, he disbanded his army at Brundisium, and proceeded with a few officers and a slender escort to the gates of Rome, before which he awaited, in the garb of an imperator, the moment when they should be opened by a decree of the senate to admit him to the glories of the triumph he had no doubt well deserved. The nobles were just at the height of their self-gratulation. Pompeius entered Italy at the moment when Catilina was being brought to bay in the Apennines. When the arch conspirator fell, they were convinced that they had nothing more to fear, and could have no further use for their victorious champion. They had just granted Lucullus the triumph which he had vainly solicited for three years. They now conceded the same reward to Metellus Creticus. They were in no hurry to associate a third commander in the honors due to the conquerors of Mithridates. They allowed Pompeius to linger outside the walls, haranging the people from time to time in the Campus Martins, trumpeting his own services, affecting to mete out praise and blame among all parties and personages, showing his own uneasiness by his jealous depreciation of Cicero, whom he regarded as a rival champion of the senate, and vainly calling for the prompt confirmation of his acts, and satisfaction of his claims to the triumph. It was not till September in the same year that this honor, so dear to every imperator, was grudgingly accorded him. He expected a solemnity of three days; the senate would indulge him with two only, and he might complain that their unworthy jealousy would not allow him to exhibit a large portion of the various spoils he had accumulated for the occasion. But he could parade a list of 800 vessels, 1,000 fortresses, and 300 cities captured, 39 cities re-peopled, 20,000 talents of gold poured into the treasury, and the tribute from foreign subjects nearly doubled, a goodlier array of services than any imperator before him.

Pompeius becomes unpopular with the senate and people.
U.C. 694. B.C. 60.

The great conqueror had now celebrated his third triumph. His first had been for victories in Africa, his second for the overthrow of Sertorius in Europe; he had now completed the illustrious cycle by inscribing on the list the name of Asia. Each section of the globe had succumbed to his prowess. Nevertheless, on descending from his car the hero found himself alone in the city in which he was wont to be thronged by friends and flatterers. Lucullus was aroused from his lethargy to attack his former rival and depreciate his services. The senate was cold or hostile; Cicero renounced the idol of his early admiration. Afranius, the consul whom Pompeius had engaged to support his interests, failed to obtain the ratification of his acts. Flavius, the tribune, sought to obtain a grant of lands for his veterans. Cato and Metellus Creticus opposed him; violence ensued, and the tribune complaining that his sanctity was outraged, dragged the consul to prison. The senators would have insisted on sharing the insult put upon their chief, but Pompeius, ashamed or alarmed, gave way once more, and withdrew his demands to a more favorable opportunity. He was deeply chagrined at the dishonor he had suffered in the eyes of his own soldiers. Repulsed by the nobles, he betook himself once more to the people, and sought to ingratiate himself with them by popular acts. They had gazed with admiration at the splendors of his triumph, and at the lavish profusion of his shows; but his magnificence was tasteless, still more did his person and demeanor lack the grace of his rival in their affections. Pompeius was no doubt in possession of great resources if he could resolve to use them himself; but he had no warm friends, no devoted followers or enthusiastic party at his back, who would volunteer their services in his behalf, and press them upon him.

CHAPTER IV.
(U.C. 693. B.C. 61.—U.C. 697. B.C. 57.)

THE FIRST TRIUMVIRATE OF CÆSAR, POMPEIUS, AND CRASSUS.

Cæsar in his province, the Further Spain.

CÆSAR had reached his fortieth year, and had never led an army under his own auspices, nor served at all, except in a subordinate rank. He had now attained the government of a province, with the command of a strong military force constantly engaged in the maintenance of the Roman occupation of Spain, and ready at any moment to be employed in the extension of the Roman territory, and the subjugation of the restless tribes on its frontier. He had two proximate objects before him–the one to relieve himself from the pressure of his debts at home, and amass a fund for future expenditure; the other to attach to his person a handful at least of officers and soldiers, to form the nucleus of a great military power. He found himself at the head of two or more legions; and the attitude of the predatory tribes of Lusitania, yet unconquered, furnished a ready pretext for action. He carried his eagles to the shores of the Atlantic, and into recesses of the country whither the Romans had never yet penetrated, driving the enemy before him through the defiles of the Herminian mountains and across the Douro and the Minho. With a rude flotilla, prepared for the service with the usual celerity of the Roman ship-builders, he assailed the rocky strongholds to which the natives had betaken themselves on the coast of Gallæcia, and could pretend that in one campaign the Further Spain was pacified even to the ocean. Through the ensuing winter he occupied himself with settling the finances of his province. He pretended to relieve the exhausted provincials from the burden of their obligations; he gave satisfaction at least to the Roman residents, their creditors. The booty he had extorted the tributes he had levied, gratified the cupidity of his officials, and he remitted large sums for the liquidation of his own debts at home. Brief as his command had been, it constituted, nevertheless, a crisis of no trifling importance in his career. It gave him confidence in his own military talents which he had never previously exercised; it gained him devoted of officers and adherents; it freed him from the stress of his pecuniary embarrassments, and it sent him back to Rome a mature aspirant to the triumph and the consulate.

Cæsar sues for the consulship.
U.C. 694. B.C. 60.

Accordingly, as the period for the elections drew near, Cæsar ventured to quit his province, in the middle of the year 60, before the arrival of a successor. He demanded a triumph for his military exploits, but he was still more anxious for the solid advantages of the consulship, for which he offered himself as a candidate. The law required that every competitor for the chief magistracy should present himself to the people on three stated occasions in the forum; whereas the imperator who still expected his triumph was not allowed in the interval to enter the city walls. This jealous regulation, which separated by so sharp a line the military character from the civil, had indeed in later times been frequently set aside, and Cæsar might fairly claim the same indulgence which had recently been conceded to Lucullus. But the nobles chose on this occasion to screen themselves behind the letter of the law for they made no doubt that Cæsar, with the vanity common to his countrymen, would forego the consulship, from which they were anxious to exclude him, and grasp at the shadowy honor of the laurel crown and gilded chariot, which they did not care to refuse. But the present claimant was not to be so trifled with. He waived his triumph, disbanded his soldiers, and paced the forum as a private citizen. The people, though baulked of the spectacle they dearly loved, acknowledged the compliment he thus paid to the value of their suffrages. There were, moreover, other interests at work to advance the suit of the popular candidate, and the nobles were obliged to content themselves with simply offering him a colleague from their own ranks.

Cæsar reconciles Crassus and Pompeius.—
The First Triumvirate. U.C. 694. B.C. 60.

Cæsar had evinced not only great self-control in his suit for this illustrious office; he had exerted the special talent he most eminently possessed, that of turning the interests of others to his own advantage, and securing for his schemes the co-operation of his own most distinguished rivals. His first care on his return to Rome was to bring together the two men whose mutual jealousy a meaner politician would have been most anxious to foster. Crassus had never forgiven Pompeius the laurels which he had so curtly plucked from him; Pompeius, having once abased the statesman by whose competition he felt himself most nearly touched, had neither the generosity nor the foresight to take him again by the hand. Baffled himself by the opposition of the senate, he had sullenly withdrawn from public affairs, and held himself aloof both from friends and enemies. It was the policy of Cæsar to overcome the mutual repulsion of two such important personages, and to open to each of them new views of ambition, in which he could assist them both conjointly. The formation of the league between these three aspirants to a dominant power in the state, which is marked as the First Triumvirate, constitutes no doubt a signal epoch in the history of the republic. It was not, indeed, like the Second Triumvirate, which succeeded at a later period, a regularly appointed board of three for the administration of affairs. It neither had, nor pretended to have, any legal basis; it was no more than a spontaneous and possibly a tacit understanding, by which the parties interested mutually bound themselves to advance the special objects of each, leaving the ultimate issue of their confederacy to the chances of the future. It constituted, in fact, in the eyes of legists and statesmen, a *"regnum"* or "tyranny", a scheme of lawless usurpation; and as such it was ever denounced by the mouths of real or pretended patriots. The application of the word regnum to this unholy combination strikes the key-note of Lucan's rhetorical poem on the civil wars which followed upon its rupture; but the conception of such a compact, fraught as it was with the gravest consequences, was due to the genius of Cæsar alone. It was by the ability and conduct of Cæsar alone that it was carried into execution; nor was he disloyal to his colleagues in carrying it out. It was to the ascendency of his own character and talents that he owed the superior fortune which abased in turn both his associates, and raised him alone to the highest pre-eminence.

CHAPTER V.
(U.C. 696. B.C. 58.—U.C. 703. B.C. 51.)

Cæsar's Conquest of Gaul.—Death of Crassus and Dissolution of the First Triumvirate.

Cæsar's conquest of Gaul.

THE narrative of the conquest of Gaul by the most consummate captain that ever led the Roman legions—a narrative related by himself in a style distinguished for its truthfulness and simplicity—must have a special interest of its own in the history of the conquering republic. Both the military tactics and the administrative policy of Rome are presented to our view in the commentaries of Cæsar on the Gallic war. We learn from this lucid record how the greatest empire of the ancient or the modern world was acquired, and how also it was organized and maintained. The commentaries are, in fact, an epitome of the history of Roman conquest. But as regards the object of the present work it will suffice to refer to them briefly as a chapter in the annals of the first triumvirate, for the light which they throw upon the aims of Cæsar and the means by which he accomplished them. The conquest and the provincial settlement of the Further Gaul occupied the proconsul without interruption from the year 696 of the city, when he entered on the command, to the year 705, when he relinquished it for the conquest of the empire. A vast amount of Roman blood and treasure was spent in his successive campaigns, but the losses of the enemy were no doubt far more exhausting. From the date of their subjugation by Cæsar the Gauls never rose again as a nation in revolt; but their pacification was due to the wise and liberal policy of their conqueror even more than to the terror of his arms.

Cæsar's first campaign. U.C. 696. B.C. 58.—He checks the movement of Helvetii.—Repulses the Suevi.

The Gauls had been in earlier times among the most formidable enemies of Rome. The citizens could never forget that the barbarians of the North had once entered and burnt their city. For a space of two centuries indeed these invaders had retreated step by step; nevertheless, from time to time they had again threatened the republic with the gravest disasters. Step by step Rome had driven them across the Apennines to the valley of the Po, and had there subdued and pacified those of their tribes that dwelt within the limits of the Alps. She had advanced by sea to the coast of Transalpine Gaul; had settled her colonies at Massilia and Aquæ Sextiæ, and had penetrated from thence still further into the interior. She had eventually organized the "Provincia," her first military dependency beyond the Alps; and to this province, which lay between the Alps and the Rhone, she had added a second, which reached from the Mediterranean to the Atlantic, and was named, from its capital, the "Narbonensis." Rome had little now to fear from the Gauls, brave and warlike as they were, for they had lost their earlier power of combination for attack or defence, and were for the most part distracted by the mutual animosity of their various tribes, and by the class jealousies of rival parties in each. The Romans could easily afford to despise the murmurs of the Allobroges, who had pretended for a moment to take a part in the revolt of Catilina. But a movement of another kind was now in progress among these northern peoples. The Helvetii had determined to make a general emigration from their own narrow and barren territory, and direct their course in a body through the centre of Gaul to the broad and fertile shores of the Atlantic. The tribes of the interior were alarmed; great disturbances might be expected to ensue. The frontiers of the Roman province itself might not be secure. It was deemed necessary to assume a high tone and forbid the movement. Cæsar hastened across the Alps, amused the Helvetii for a few days with negotiations while he fortified the banks of the Rhone which they proposed to cross below Geneva, and forced them to take a difficult route to the northward, and plunge into the country of the Ædui in the centre of Gaul. Upon this track he quickly followed them, routed them first on the banks of the Saône, and thence pursued them to the neighborhood of Bibracte (Autun), where he finally crushed them. From thence he turned his arms against the Suevi, a German tribe, who, under their chief, Ariovistus, had crossed the Rhine on a predatory incursion, and approached Vensontio (Besançon). Having relieved the more quiet and settled communities of Gaul from both these invaders, he set himself to form an alliance with some and sow dissensions among others, so as to prepare the way, in accordance with the usual policy of the Roman conquerors, for the eventual subjugation of all.

Cæsar's second campaign against the Belgic tribes.—Third Campaign against the Veneti.—Fourth campaign: crossing of the Rhine and invasion of Britain. U.C. 699. B.C. 55.—Second descent on Britain. U.C. 700.

The Ædui and Averni in the centre of Gaul, the Remi in the north-east, were disposed, each with selfish views of their own, to aid in the ruin of their common country, while they hailed Cæsar as their protector against the restless Germans on their eastern frontier. In the second Belgic year of his command (U.C. 697) the proconsul broke the confederacy of the Belgic tribes on the Meuse and the Moselle. In his next campaign (698) he worsted the naval power of the Veneti in Armorica, and reduced for the most part the coast of the Channel, while his lieutenants were equally successful in overcoming the tribes of Aquitania. In the year 699 Gaul was very generally pacified; but the legions required to be kept in exercise; their officers were greedy of more plunder. Cæsar had a great military engine to form and to maintain, and he did not scruple as to the means to be employed. He advanced beyond the limits of his province, threw a bridge across the broad and rapid Rhine—the greatest effort of the kind yet accomplished by the Roman forces—and penetrated for an instant into the German forests. This incursion indeed had no result. Cæsar turned in another direction. In the autumn of the same year he made a descent with two legions upon the coast of Britain. Having beaten the natives of the Kentish territory in some slight encounters, but suffered at the same time much injury to his vessels from tides and storms, he withdrew hastily into winter quarters in Gaul. In no way discouraged, however, he again attacked the Britons in the succeeding summer, and after beating down the opposing forces, effected the passage of the Thames at a ford above London. There is reason to believe that he penetrated into the interior as far as Verulamium, in Hertfordshire. An important discovery of coins of Julius Cæsar seems to indicate that a detachment at least of his forces was for a moment advanced some miles to the north of that spot. But he did not care to effect a permanent lodgment in our island, which would have weakened his position in Gaul. He was content to retire with the promise of a slender tribute, and this was probably never paid after his departure. He had occupied his troops, he had amused the people at Rome, who listened with delight to their hero's despatches, and he had allowed affairs at home to ripen for the crisis to which, through his partizans, he was gradually urging them.

Cæsar concerts with the triumvirs at Lucca.—An extraordinary commission assigned to Pompeius. U.C. 697. B.C. 57.—Proposed restoration of the king of Egypt. U.C. 698. B.C. 56.—Disturbances in the city.

During the progress of his campaigns the proconsul's vigilance had indeed never been entirely diverted from the march of events in the city. After each season of military operations he had repaired to the baths of Lucca, at the southern limit of his province—for the laws forbade an imperator to enter Italy while retaining his command—and there had concerted, with the friends who flocked to him from Rome, the measures most conducive to their common interests. During his absence the bands of the triumvirate had become relaxed. Pompeius and Crassus, always cold to one another, were pursuing their own private objects, each hastening as he thought to the attainment of supreme power. Cicero had attached himself to Pompeius; and, a scarcity of corn occurring, he moved that an extraordinary commission should be assigned to his patron for supplying the necessities of the capital. The republic had now become familiar with these monopolies of power. The consuls assented, and for the third time Pompeius was placed above the laws. He was authorized to demand supplies from any part of the empire, and to fix the prices at his own discretion. The officers to be employed, and enriched by the employment, were to be appointed by himself; his powers were to be continued for five years. Cicero himself accepted a place on assigned to the commission. The whole scheme was a mere pretence for putting the great captain at the helm of state which four years before he had unwarily abandoned. But Pompeius, from carelessness or incapacity, failed to gain any accession of strength from the powers thus thrust upon him. With ample means of encouraging his friends and purchasing his enemies, he found himself more than ever exposed to the intrigues of the nobles and the violence of the mob. He was defeated in suing for a further appointment which now offered itself as a prize for contending factions. The republic seems to have postponed the acceptance of the king of Egypt's legacy. The story of this legacy is indeed obscure and doubtful. The reigning sovereign, Ptolemæus Auletes, had at this juncture been expelled by his subjects, and the senate proposed to restore him. The public man to whom this business should be committed would require the command of an army, and doubtless would reap for himself fame, power, and emolument. The government desired to send one of their own party. The consular Lentulus and some tribunes in the interest of Pompeius interposed, alleging an oracle of the Sibyl to the effect that the king must not be restored "with a multitude;" a phrase which was deemed to preclude the use of an armed force. Lentulus was baffled; the appointment, army and all, was still open. But when Pompeius, through his creatures, demanded it for himself, he could succeed no better. The turbulence of the popular demagogues rendered any decision impossible. The city became once more a prey to internal tumults; the nobles threw themselves again on the support of their licentious champion, Milo. At such critical moments omens are never wanting to stir the popular feeling. The statue of Jupiter on the Alban mount was struck with lightning, an event which caused general consternation, as a presage of impending calamity. Clodius seems to have sown dissension between Pompeius and Crassus. At the same time the senate was emboldened to talk of recalling Cæsar from his province, and ex posing him, unarmed, to impeachment and exile, or even death.

Cæsar again at Lucca. U.C. 698. B.C. 56.
Impending crisis of the free-state.

Towards the close of the year 698 the proconsul had repaired, as in the previous winter, to his station at Lucca; and thither consulars and officials of all ranks flocked from the city to meet him. A hundred and twenty lictors might be counted at his door, while two hundred senators, nearly one-half of the whole order, paid their court at his receptions. All these magnates returned to Rome charmed with his affable manners and his full-handed generosity. All were rapidly coming to the conclusion that the reign of equal law was approaching its end, to he succeeded by the ascendency of a popular hero. The fatal crisis had indeed almost arrived. The machinery of the free-state could perform its functions no longer. The consuls and tribunes, the senate and the people, mutually checked each other's movements, and paralyzed the action of the body politic. The elections for the ensuing year were impeded, the consuls interposing under pretence of adverse auspices, and forbidding the tribes to assemble. Meanwhile they abstained in person from all the duties of their office, clad themselves in mourning, refrained from the spectacles and from the solemn festival on the Alban mount, as men under constraint of the mob and deprived of their legitimate power. When at last the consuls' chairs became vacant no successors had been duly appointed. The year 699 opened with an interregnum. While riot reigned at home there could be little check upon license abroad. Gabinius, as proconsul of Syria, took upon himself to set Ptolemæus on his throne at Alexandria, in defiance of the recent veto of the senate. Meanwhile, the impatient candidates, disregarding the legal forms of an interregnum, induced the tribunes to convene the people irregularly. While the nobles employed bribery for their nominee Domitius, the younger Crassus arrived from Gaul with a detachment of Cæsar's veterans, and overbore all opposition. The new consuls, Pompeius and Crassus, having thus obtained their appointment by violence, secured the other offices for their friends by similar outrage. Cato, who had returned from his mission to Cyprus without stain of pecuniary corruption, now sued for the prætorship, but was mortified by a rejection, which was rendered doubly vexatious by the infamy of Vatinius, whom the triumvirs exalted over his head.

Cæsar's command extended for a second term of five years.
U.C. 700. B.C. 54.—Death of Julia.

Cæsar had induced his colleagues to smother their mutual jealousies. He next secured for them, by the intervention of the tribune Trebonius, the important provinces of Spain and Syria on their descent from office. In return he obtained, through their assistance, the extension of his own command for a second period of five years. They could urge that the regions which he had so quickly conquered were but half pacified, and as yet imperfectly organized. Cæsar himself looked forward to confirming his influence over his legions, while he anticipated the decline of his rivals' power in the interval. The resistance of the nobles to a measure which proved so fatal to them was petulant rather than determined. Cato, who had lost much of his authority by daily collision with violence and vulgarity, and Favonius, a party brawler rather than a political leader, were the most active champions of a faction from which Lucullus, Servilius, and Lentulus now held themselves aloof. The tribunes on different sides engaged in the petty warfare of obstructing public ways and locking the doors of civic buildings. Cato got himself lifted on men's shoulders in order to force his way into the place of meeting, and employed the stale trick of declaring the auspices adverse. He was answered by the brandishing of clubs and showers of stones; swords and daggers were drawn in the affray, and the friends of the optimates were driven from the arena, not without bloodshed. Such were the tumultuous proceedings by which the desperate policy of the triumvirs was ratified. It was in one of these scenes of violence that the robe of Pompeius became sprinkled with blood. On his return home thus disfigured he was met by his youthful consort Julia, who was alarmed for his safety. Horrified at the sight, she was seized with premature labor, and died from its effects shortly afterwards.

Relative position of the triumvirs at this period. U.C. 700. B.C. 54.— Crassus proconsul in Syria. U.C. 700. B.C. 54.— Battle of Carrhæ. U.C. 701. B.C. 53.

Pompeius, notwithstanding his coldness in public affairs, was a man of strong domestic sensibility. The loss of his young wife affected him deeply, and made him perhaps more than ever supine and sluggish in the prosecution of his interests. He might otherwise have turned to good account an event which cut through the entanglements of his personal connection with his rival. The supereminent position he now enjoyed, as the head of an important commission, and the chief of a large army which he could command from beneath the walls of Rome, gave him an immense advantage over Cæsar, who was engaged, at a great distance, in a long and still precarious warfare; and over

Crassus also, who at the same moment was rushing blindly upon an arduous expedition. Cæsar had conquered the Gauls, and could pretend that he had received their submission; but the Belgic tribes were again in arms, and his enemies at home might anticipate at any moment his defeat or death. Crassus, in undertaking the government of Syria, had announced his intention of making war upon the Parthians; and he, too, now advanced in years and long disused to arms, might soon succumb to a formidable foe in a difficult country. The nobles, indeed, who had little fear of him at home, were jealous of his possible success abroad, and induced one of the tribunes to denounce his enterprise as a national crime, and stir up the superstitious feelings of the people against it. But Crassus was not deterred by the direful omens which were said to attend his exit from the city. On arriving at the seat of his government he directed the advance of troops to the Euphrates. He entered the region of Osrhoene, captured some towns, and placed in them Roman garrisons, before he returned to his headquarters for the winter. When the Parthian government complained of this unprovoked aggression upon their dependency, the proconsul replied that he would give them an answer in their capital, Seleucia. As soon as he had completed his preparations, he led a force of several legions across the desolate and arid district between the Euphrates and the Tigris. The Parthians had determined to let him advance to a certain distance unopposed; they had directed an officer of their own to offer his services as guide, and lead him into the ambush which they had prepared for him. The Roman troops had become exhausted and demoralized under a chief in whom they had no confidence. When they turned back disheartened, the Parthians closed around them with their clouds of light cavalry, and inflicted upon them disastrous losses. At last the Romans sustained a crushing defeat under the walls of Carrhæ. The son of Crassus, a gallant young officer from Cæsar's army, was slain; and the proconsul, stricken with grief and shame, deemed it more prudent to negotiate than to hazard a rapid flight. The Parthians deceived and entrapped him, and Crassus himself was slain in a futile attempt at rescue the main body of his army was captured, and carried away into the interior. A small remnant only was saved by the prompt vigor of C. Cassius Longinus, and led back within the frontiers of Syria. The overthrow of Carrhæ was one of the gravest disasters ever sustained by the Roman arms. It is said that 20,000 were slain and 10,000 carried into captivity.

The officers were treated with scorn and mockery; the head of Crassus was cut off, and molten gold, according to the story, was poured into the mouth of the most avaricious of the Romans; but the captives seem to have been treated with indulgence and allowed to settle in the land of their conquerors.

Cæsar's peril in Gaul: sixth year of the Gallic war. U.C. 701. B.C. 53.

The mass of the citizens at home appear to have regarded this discomfiture with comparative indifference; so little was Crassus loved or respected among them; so distant was the scene of operations. It was not till a later period, and under other political circumstances, that so signal a defeat was deemed to demand an equally signal reparation. Doubtless, the eyes of nobles and people became more intently fixed on the position of the proconsul of Gaul, which was becoming more and more hazardous. On his return from his second expedition into Britain, Cæsar had found Gaul tranquil and apparently resigned to the yoke. He held a meeting of the states at Samarobriva (Amiens), his northern capital, and assured himself of their fidelity. He had intended to spend the winter at Lucca. But meanwhile the tribes between the Loire and the Rhine had concerted a wide conspiracy, and only waited for the proconsul's departure to rise in arms. Their revolt was accidentally precipitated, and Cæsar was still at hand but, cooped up in his own quarters, he remained for some time ignorant of the imminent danger to which his outlying detachments were exposed. Q. Cicero, the orator's brother, was at the head of one of these, and could with difficulty notify his peril to his chief by a billet, inscribed with Greek characters, shot into his camp. The vigor and genius of Cæsar now prevailed. He restored tranquillity among the great mass of the insurgent peoples; he made a signal example of the Eburones, a tribe of Cimbric origin, whom he delivered over as aliens to the blind hostility of the Gauls around them; and with the defeat of the warlike Treviri he seemed to have accomplished a second and final pacification of the province. But his peril had been great; his conquests were evidently incomplete; his position was precarious. Both his friends and enemies at Rome might equally doubt whether he would survive the prolongation of his foreign adventure.

Ascendancy of Pompeius in the senate.—
Milo slays Clodius. U.C. 702. B.C. 52.

The year of the defeat of Carrhæ and the sudden insurrection of the Gauls had again opened at Rome with an interregnum, which lasted for more than six months. The flagrant bribery practised by the candidates for office had induced the best of the senators and of the tribunes to combine in preventing the assembling of the comitia. At last Cato himself became alarmed, and urged Pompeius to assume the functions of a dictator and demand an election. The triumvir, released from his connection with one colleague, and apprized, perhaps, of the fresh embarrassment of the other, gladly drew near to the party of the optimates. He interposed to procure the election of two chiefs of their faction, Calvinus and Messala, and the nobles hailed him once again as the champion of their special interests. The calm, however, which succeeded was of short duration. The elections for the ensuing year were again thwarted; the year 702 opened, like the preceding, with an interregnum. Assuredly Pompeius could have controlled the disorder; but he seems rather to have assisted it. Milo, Scipio, and Hypsæus demanded each the consulship with arms in their hands; every day was marked with fresh riot, and blood was frequently shed. But amidst the obscure murders which marked this era of violence and ferocity, there was one which caused especial sensation, and demanded stronger measures of repression. It happened that in the month of January of this year, Milo was journeying on the Appian Way, accompanied in his carriage by his wife, and attended by a retinue of servants, and, as was his wont, by a troop of gladiators. Near to Bovillæ, a few miles from the city, he was met by Clodius, who was on horseback, with a small company of armed men around him. It does not appear that the affray which ensued was premeditated, for to travel with armed attendants was not unusual, and both Milo and Clodius were men who might apprehend the violence which they had themselves often provoked. But a quarrel ensued between their respective escorts, and Clodius, wounded in the struggle, took refuge in a roadside holstelry. Milo, giving way to his fury, attacked the house, and caused his enemy to be dragged forth and slain. The corpse lay in the road till it was picked up by a passing friend and brought to the city. Here it was exposed to the gaze of the multitude, who worked themselves into frenzy at the sight. A riot broke out; benches, books, and papers were snatched from the curia in which the senate was wont to assemble, fire was set to the pile, and the flames which consumed the remains of Clodius spread from house to house over a considerable space bordering on the forum. The rioters proceeded to attack the mansions of several nobles, and particularly that of Milo himself. He was prepared, however, for the attempt, and repulsed the assailants with bloodshed. The knights and senators armed their clients to suppress the commotion, and quiet was at last restored after several days of uproar and violence.

Pompeius appointed sole consul.
U.C. 702. B.C. 52.

The disorder of public affairs had thus reached a crisis which demanded exceptional measures for the public security. Men of peace who dared not yet insist upon the appointment of a dictator, men who still clung to the vain shadow of constitutional forms, men such as Cicero, fled from the city where there was no longer a people or a senate, where the mob held the streets and the tribunals were impotent or corrupt. The great parties which had formerly represented social interests had lapsed into mere factions of families or classes, which sought power for the sake of public plunder. Few honest patriots still continued to haunt the forum, or obtrude themselves upon the cabals of selfish oligarchs. Cato himself, as we have seen, though unshaken in courage, despaired of the ancient principles of the commonwealth. Liberty, he saw, was menaced by two dangers, within by anarchy, without by usurpation; and when he looked around for a defender he found, even among those whom Cicero had designated as the party of the "good men," so much cowardice and self-interest, that he at last determined to demand from an individual that protection for the state which the laws could no longer assure to her. "Better," he said, "to choose our own master than to wait for the tyrant whom anarchy will impose upon us." But there remained in fact no choice in the matter. There was as yet only one master at whose feet Rome could throw herself. With bitter mortification Bibulus proposed, after an interregnum of nearly three months, the appointment of Pompeius as sole consul, and Cato supported him. They might hope that, content with this pre-eminence, which was less odious than that of dictator, though in fact even less known to the laws, the great man would restore order in the city, and find means for compelling the proconsul of Gaul to surrender his province and disband his formidable armies, The repression of scandalous disorders, the overthrow of a licentious ambition, might, after all, it seemed, be cheaply purchased by one year of despotism. Pompeius was old in years, supine and vain; possibly he might be used for the occasion, and thrown away afterwards. But if such was the secret reasoning of the despairing chiefs of the senate, they did not consider how surely the precedent which they were about to set would give occasion and color to further attempts, and pave the way to the inevitable monarchy.

Trial of Milo.

The sole consul entered upon his irregular office in a month irregularly intercalated, for the calendar of the year had long fallen into confusion, and, like the state, required vigorous measures of amendment. "Kind as kings upon their coronation day," he vowed that he would take Cato as his adviser, and rule the state in the interests of freedom. He had taken no counsel with Cæsar in the matter. He now finally cast off the bonds of alliance with his late associate, and devoted himself to the policy of the optimates, which he had long felt to be properly his own. Twice already be had achieved the lead of their party, and twice he had sacrificed it to the pride of standing aloof from all connection with men whom he deemed his inferiors in influence and ability. The consulship, which he now held without a colleague, raised him above all the citizens in dignity; but his proconsular imperium was far more valuable to him from the actual power which it lodged in his hands. He commanded legions in Spain and cohorts at the gates of the city, and these he would never suffer to be wrested from him, while he was prepared to insist on Cæsar's return, unarmed, to the city. Meanwhile he was content to sur render Milo to the demands of the populace. The culprit, arraigned before a select body of eighty-one judices, enlisted Cicero in his defence. The great orator prepared to assert his client's innocence, and exult in the bold act of self-defence which had freed the commonwealth from a danger and a pest. But when he rose to speak he was greeted by furious shouts, and was at the same time put out of countenance by the display of an armed force which Pompeius had introduced into the forum to overawe him. He stammered through a short and nerveless oration, and sat down with his task only half finished. Milo, convicted of murder, was allowed to retire into exile, and chose Massilia for his retreat. On returning home, Cicero composed for publication the speech he should have delivered in his defence. The story is told that his vanity prompted him to send to his client the splendid declamation he had penned; and that Milo replied with a sneer, not wholly undeserved, that he deemed himself fortunate that so convincing an argument had not been actually delivered; "else," he said, "I should not now be enjoying the delicious mullets of this place."

Seventh year of the Gallic war. U.C. 702. B.C. 52.—Gallant resistance of Vercingetorix.—Final conquest of Gaul. U.C. 703. B.C. 51.

Pompeius was now at the height of his fortunes. He enjoyed all but the name of royalty. The armed bands which had kept the city in an uproar were speedily dispersed; tranquillity was restored; abundance was secured; the nobles acquiesced, and the people were satisfied. The only rival he had cause to fear was far away and en tangled in increasing difficulties. Cæsar had barely escaped from the last attack of his revolted subjects, and he was now held in so little awe by his adversaries at home, that on the occasion of an act of perfidy, which might not unjustly be imputed to him, in his dealings with the public enemy, Cato had not scrupled to demand that he should be delivered up to the Gauls to save, as he pretended, the honor of the republic. The demand, indeed, was refused or evaded; but it might give him a significant hint of the bitterness of his enemies and the insecurity of his position at home. At the close of the year 53, after the second pacification of his province, he had repaired, as usual, for the winter to Lucca to watch events in Italy; but fresh plots were in agitation among the Gauls. It was in the centre of their country, between the Seine and the Garonne, that the flame burst forth and spread rapidly. It was kindled by the Druids, the religious caste which was powerful among the Carnutes, and was closely connected with the ruling classes throughout the country. At Genabus (Orleans, or rather Gien), on the Loire, the Roman traders had established themselves in considerable numbers; for the traffic of the north and south followed the track of the great streams, and the bend which that river makes in the middle of its course formed a central point of communication between them. The native population rose; the foreigners were surprised and massacred. The command of a general revolt was taken by Vercingetorix, a chief of the Arverni, the only name among the Gauls which attained to any distinction in these wars, and that a title, perhaps, rather than a personal appellative. But the man who bore it deserves to be better known to us, for even in the commentaries of his enemy he stands forth as a great military genius, and the struggle which he maintained, however brief, was one of the most critical in the Roman military annals. Under his command the Gauls inflicted a notable disaster upon the invader at Gergovia, struck his own sword from his hand, and cut off his retreat into Italy. In this, indeed, Vercingetorix was only too successful. To escape from the Gauls would have been to fall into the hands of the enemy at home. Had the victor left Cæsar but a loophole for retreat, he might have been rid of him for ever. There was, however, no alternative for him but to conquer beyond the Alps, or be crushed within them. But his forces were still numerous to the north of the Seine; his lieutenant Labienus checked and worsted the tribes by which he was himself there assailed, and was enabled to join his chief, and sustain him against the attack of the populations that were rising behind him. Another engagement ensued, and Cæsar was this time victorious. Vercingetorix led his routed followers to Alesia, near the modern Dijon, which he invested with a force of 80,000 warriors. Cæsar pursued him, and completed another circumvallation, in which be enclosed these vast numbers, together with a multitude of unarmed fugitives, who perished with hunger between the two contending armies. The forces of Vercingetorix, after divers attempts to break through the blockading lines, were at last reduced by famine. Their gallant leader offered himself as a sacrifice for them, and the lives of his people were spared; but he was himself ungenerously carried off, and reserved for the future triumph of the conqueror, and the cruel death of a Pontius and a Perseus. The crisis had passed; the subjugation of the whole region between the Alps, the Rhine, and the ocean was completed in the following year, the eighth of Cæsar's proconsulship; and the spirit of insurrection was daunted, perhaps, by the unrelenting severity with which he chastised it. In eight campaigns he had taken, as Plutarch has recorded, more than 800 cities, worsted 300 nations, and encountered three millions of men in arms, of whom he had slain one million and made an equal number of prisoners.

Feeble measures of Pompeius.

Secure as he felt himself in his position at the head of affairs, Pompeius had been unable to conceive any large measures for the public weal. He had provided, by means of the extensive powers committed to him, for the supply of the city with corn; but he had not attempted to grapple with the great economical difficulties of the day, under which the mass of the citizens was sinking into poverty and degradation. The planting of colonies, the introduction of foreigners to the privileges of the state, the relief of debtors oppressed by hard laws and still harder usages, were matters which he left to be dealt with by one who should rise hereafter to the true spirit of the dictators of old. His laws against bribery, and other specious political measures, were mere palliative expedients. Nor did he care to observe even these in his own conduct. He had interdicted the eulogies which the powerful friends of a culprit had been allowed to utter before his judges; but when Metellus Scipio, a magnate of the highest standing, whose daughter he had recently espoused, was cited before a tribunal, he condescended to speak himself in his favor, and thereby extort an acquittal. He had obtained a decree that no magistrate should enjoy a province till five years after quitting his office at home; but this enactment, which, however important, was impossible of execution, he promptly violated in his own case, by causing his proconsulship to be prolonged for a second term, even while he was himself actually consul. Again, he had appointed that no man should sue for a public charge while absent from the city. The rule was intended no doubt as a check upon Cæsar; but he had become jealous of his rival's military achievements, and when he found it for his own interest to facilitate Cæsar's election to a second consulship, in order to draw him prematurely from his command in Gaul, he made an exception to this law also.

Cæsar's organization of Gaul.

The final reduction of Gaul found the work of pacification already far advanced. Cæsar's policy differed from that of former governors. The provinces on either side of the Alps had been placed under the control of garrisons and colonies. Portions of their soil had been conferred upon such

Roman citizens as would exchange security at home for lands to be maintained at the risk of their own lives abroad. But the ancient policy of the republic could not be extended to the vast territories which. Cæsar had now to organize. Nor was it his wish to bring Rome, as it were, into the provinces; his object was rather to introduce the Gaulish foreigners into Rome, and give them an interest in the city of their conquerors. The first step towards making them citizens was to lighten for them the Roman yoke. Accordingly he established among them no badges of subjection in the shape of colonies. He left them their realms and territories as well as their laws and their religion. He allowed to most of them a specious show of freedom. They retained their magistrates and senates, guided no doubt by Roman agents. The tribute required of the provincials was softened by the title of military assessment. Honors and privileges were showered upon their chiefs and cities. But, after all, the manner of the magnanimous Roman won as many hearts as his benefactions. When he saw the sword which had been snatched from him in his battle with the Arverni suspended in the temple of its captors, he refused to reclaim it, saying, with a gracious smile, that the offering was sacred.

Cæsar organizes his military resources in Gaul.

But Cæsar had yet another enemy within the bounds of his wide dominion. The senate, towards whom his position had become one of open defiance, had established a stronghold of its own interests in the cities of the Narbonensis. From the time that Pompeius had led his legions through that country against Sertorius, driving the remnant of the Marians before him, the south of Gaul had been filled with the agents of the senatorial party, and its resources applied to the furtherance of their policy. Since his return to Rome Pompeius had continued, in fact, to govern the district by the hands of Fonteius and other proconsuls up to the time of Cæsar's appointment. The new governor had set himself to undo the work of his predecessors. He exerted himself to recover the favor of the Massilians, by extending the strip of territory which they were allowed to hold in nominal independence. He rewarded his faithful adherents, both Roman and provincial, with lands and largesses, and placed the government of the country in their hands. Meanwhile he kept his legions ready for future service. Every cohort, stationed far or near, became a depôt for the enlistment of the most warlike of the natives, whose military spirit prompted them to attach themselves to the service of so gallant and generous a captain. The soldiers, indeed, with whom he had effected the conquest had themselves been principally of Gaulish blood; the republic had furnished him with no troops from Italy, and a contingent which he had borrowed from Pompeius he had promptly surrendered when it was demanded of him, and trusted himself solely to his own levies. The legions numbered the Seventh, Eighth, and Ninth, which he had found in the Cisalpine at the outset of his career, were probably the forces raised by Metellus in that region, when he closed the Alps against Catilina. The Tenth legion had been formed by his predecessors in the Transalpine to control the Allobroges. The Eleventh and Twelfth were the proconsul's own hasty conscription within the two provinces at the commencement of his first campaign against the Helvetii. The Thirteenth and Fourteenth he enlisted also in Gaul to oppose the great confederacy of the Belgians.

Cæsar's levies in Gaul.

Of these the latter had been cut in pieces by the Eburones; but another Fourteenth and a Fifteenth also were afterwards levied in the Gaulish territories. A small portion only of these warriors could have been of genuine Roman or Italian extraction; they were mainly drawn, no doubt, from the native population of the states which had been endowed with the "rights of Latium," and thus placed by special favor on a footing of subordinate or incomplete citizenship. The legions, however, thus semi-Romanized, were attended by numerous foreign cohorts, equipped with similar arms, and trained under the same discipline. The common dangers and glories of a few campaigns, side by side, had rendered these auxiliaries no less efficient than their regular comrades. One entire legion Cæsar did not scruple to compose of Gauls only. The helmets of these soldiers were distinguished by the figure of a lark or a tuft of its plumage, whence the legion itself derived its name *Alauda*. The bird was itself no bad representative of the noisy and vivacious people who were proud to accept it as their symbol. They were glad, perhaps, to escape from the patriarchal tyranny of their priests and nobles, and put themselves under a discipline, which, however stern, was congenial to their military instincts. They admired and loved the generous leader who sought to gain the personal attachment of his warriors as no Roman imperator had cared to do before him. Among Cæsar's contemporaries it was remarked that throughout his Gallic campaigns his soldiers never mutinied. Their cheerful endurance of toils and privations more dismayed the enemy than their well-known prowess in the field. They could never be induced, when captured, to turn their arms against him, while Pompeius and Lucullus, it was said, had constantly been confronted by renegades from their own ranks. Gaul had been conquered under Cæsar by the Gauls themselves, and it was perhaps the greatest of their conquests hitherto. They had indeed gained a triumph over Rome in earlier times; but the triumph had been signally reversed and never yet repeated. The day was coming when they were about to conquer Rome once for all, and establish the throne of the Cæsars upon a lasting foundation.

CHAPTER VI.
(U.C. 703. B.C. 51.—U.C. 705. B.C. 49.)

RUPTURE BETWEEN CÆSAR AND THE SENATE.

Cæsar's position assailed by the senatorial party.

AT the end of six months, Pompeius, following the prescriptive rule of the dictatorial office, divested himself of his sole consulship, and caused his father-in-law, Metellus Scipio, to be associated with him. He had succeeded in imposing order upon the populace in the city; he had given the tribunals a semblance at least of purity and justice, and the senate might seem to recover under his shelter some portion of its pristine dignity. To maintain this outward show he obtained the consulship for the next year for two of its leading members, Servius Sulpicius, a moderate man and of high character, and M. Marcellus, a violent aristocrat devoted to his patron's personal interests, while he procured the defeat of Cato, whom he regarded as a troublesome interloper. Cæsar had just effected the destruction of Vercingetorix, and the people had constrained the senate to decree a "supplication" or public thanksgiving in his honor. Marcellus retorted by gravely demanding that the proconsul of Gaul should be recalled. The fiercest partisans of the oligarchy, confident in the pre-eminent position now occupied by Pompeius, supported him vehemently; but their violence disturbed their own champion who feared a renewal of the recent tumults, and this desperate measure was overruled. The enemies of Cæsar found other ways of venting their displeasure. The proconsul had accepted the patronage of the Transpadane Gauls and had founded a colony at Novum Comum, the modern Como. The Transpadanes had already acquired from Pompeius Strabo the "rights of Latium," which at this time conferred almost the consideration, as well as many of the privileges, of the Roman franchise. Marcellus, in order to irritate Cæsar, had caused a citizen of this Latin colony to be seized on some pretence, and beaten with rods. The man was not a Roman, indeed, nor had he served, it would seem, a magistracy in his own town, by which he would have acquired the immunities of a Roman. Marcellus may not have violated the actual letter of the law, which exempted a Roman citizen from the degradation of the scourge; nevertheless, the Romans themselves acknowledged that it was an indignity to scourge even a Latin, and both Cæsar and his friends in the city regarded the act as a deliberate affront to the popular chieftain.

Cicero proconsul of Cilicia.
U.C. 703. B.C. 51.

Cæsar, with studied moderation, refrained from resenting this high-handed proceeding. He knew that the insolence of the nobles was confirming him in the favor of the populace. Nor, indeed, did Pompeius give it his august countenance. Possibly he, too, was content to let the citizens mark the difference between a sage and experienced champion such as himself, and the vulgar violence of the headstrong faction to which he had given their turn of office. He absented himself from Rome during the remainder of the year, and visited his villas, pretending to be employed in provisioning the city. While his rival was completing, in his eighth campaign, the long war which formed his army and created his resources, he withdrew with his intimates from the more eminent men of his party, dallied with the pursuits of literature and philosophy, and sought perhaps to recruit his failing health. Meanwhile the nobles, as if bent on their own ruin, strove to remove the man from whose moderation they might still have learnt a salutary lesson. They had persuaded Cicero to quit, not without reluctance, the centre of affairs, and assume the government of Cilicia from the month of August in this year. Discarded as he had long been from the councils of the optimates, and treated with ill-disguised contempt by the brawlers who swayed them, he still clung to the hope that all classes would at last combine to invoke him to save the state a second time. But the spirit of the senatorial faction was such that he would have been allowed to do them no service had he remained within their call, while his short career as proconsul in Cilicia had obtained for him well-merited honor. In the conduct of his civil administration in that province he left a brilliant example of honor and integrity; and even in the command of a military force against the marauders in the mountains, he demeaned himself, though untrained in arms, as became a Roman imperator. His opportunities, however, were slight, and his successes were necessarily trifling. The innate vanity of his character is again curiously evinced by the dream in which he indulged, that he had merited the glories of a legitimate triumph, which on his return he solicited with unworthy importunity.

Cæsar secures support by bribery.

The consul M. Marcellus had urged Cæsar's peremptory recall. Pompeius, who had himself obtained leave for him to sue for the consulship without quitting his government, gave way so far as to allow the senate to decree at the end of September in this year that a successor to his province should be definitely appointed six months from that time, that is, in the March following. No policy could be more feeble than this. It irritated Cæsar; at the same time it gave him an interval to provide for his own defence. Two of the tribunes sprang forward to put their veto upon the decree. The consul Sulpicius himself exclaimed against it. It seems that even at this moment of embittered feeling many of the more respect able members of the senate demurred to an act so violent and indecent. Pompeius, who had just quitted the city under pretence of hastening to repair to his province, watched every turn in the game, and now affected to disapprove of so extreme a measure. He allowed C. Marcellus, the cousin of Marcus, to be elected consul for the ensuing year, thus securing one strong partisan to the senate; but he neutralized this act of vigor to some extent by getting Paulus Æmilius appointed his colleague, who was well known to have sold himself to Cæsar for a large sum of money with which to erect his splendid basilica in the forum. Among the new tribunes was another friend of Cæsar, who was also reputed to have been bought with Gallic gold. C. Scribonius Curio was the son of a senator of high rank and authority, a firm but temperate supporter of his party. The son had early disgraced himself by his licentiousness, he had found himself companions among the most dissolute young men of his class; he was needy and unprincipled. Yet he was a youth not only of excellent parts but also of amiable character. He was a favorite with Cicero, who, despairing of his own contemporaries, now often looked with pleasing enthusiasm to the rising generation for objects of hope and faith. But he was not proof against Cæsar's seductions, and now, having attained an important office, he was prepared to defend his cause with desperate resolution.

The senate strengthen their military resources.

Cæsar's enemies were no doubt well aware of the sums he had lavished in the purchase of adherents. Far more lavish was the expenditure which he incurred in the organization of his province strengthen and his armies. Disappointed in their hope that he might be crushed by the Gauls, they now flattered themselves that his resources were exhausted, that they could outbid him in the favor of the provincials and even of his own soldiers. When Atticus the Epicurean, who looked more to money than to politics, called on him for the liquidation of a private debt of fifty talents, they imagined that he would be seriously embarrassed. He repaid this trifling blow by ordering the construction of a sumptuous villa at Aricia. Above all, they placed their reliance on the force of seven legions which were under the command of Pompeius, and which, though quartered in Spain, might be promply transported across the sea, even if the route of Gaul should be closed against them. At this moment the commander in Syria was calling for reinforcements against the Parthians. The senate decreed that two additional legions should be sent to him. The resources of the republic lay in the rival camps of Pompeius and Cæsar. The senate demanded a legion from each. Pompeius, as has been before mentioned, had previously lent a legion to Cæsar; this he now required to be returned to him for his own contingent, while the senate insisted on his furnishing another for his own. Two divisions were thus removed from Gaul, and when they arrived in Italy the senate unscrupulously retained them near the frontier to strengthen their own position. But Cæsar had plied them with generous gifts, and in the end they imparted weakness rather than strength to his enemies. Meanwhile these untoward consequences were little foreseen by Pompeius or the faction which clamored around him. When they discussed among themselves their chances of success and some one inquired of their champion what he would do should their enemy persist in suing for the consulship, and refuse at the same time to relinquish his command—"What," he replied, "if my own son should raise his stick against me!"

Curio baffles the motion for Cæsar's recall.
U.C. 704. B.C. 50.

The first two months of the year 50 B.C. were occupied with the reception of foreign embassies and the regulation of external affairs. On the 1st of March the question arose, which had been suspended since the previous September, and on which the existence of the commonwealth itself depended. Cæsar's powers were destined to expire on the last day of December, B.C. 49; but the nobles were too impatient to wait still nearly two years for this much-looked-for consummation. Delay, which at a previous time might have involved him in further risks, could now, since the final pacification of his province, serve only to strengthen his position. The recent motion for his recall had been thus far evaded. C. Marcellus now came forward to agitate it afresh. But Paulus temporized, Curio threatened; Pompeius, it would seem, had been taken with a cold fit of timidity, or, at least, of procrastination. Common decency required, perhaps, that an interval of some months should be accorded, and Marcellus was constrained to extend the respite till the November next ensuing. With this proviso a majority of the senate would have voted for Cæsar's recall, notwithstanding the silence of the other consul. But Curio now rose in his place, and in a speech conciliatory indeed, and flattering towards Marcellus himself, insinuated that if such a course were adopted towards Cæsar, the same measure must in fairness be applied to Pompeius also. If this second resolution were rejected, he vowed to put his veto on the first. Marcellus now lost all command of his temper. He denounced Cæsar as a brigand, and urged the senate to declare him a public enemy unless he should lay down his arms. But Curio had taken counsel with his friends, and was well assured that his specious proposal would be strongly supported. He insisted that the question should be put to the vote, and when the senators were counted off on the opposite sides of the hall, the motion for the simultaneous disarming of both the rivals was carried by an overwhelming majority. Curio was content with this result, which he knew he could turn to the interest of his patron. The people received him in the forum with redoubled acclamations, and strewed his path with flowers in acknowledgment of the substantial victories he had gained. It was certain that Pompeius would not surrender his legions, and Cæsar would become justly entitled to retain his own command. Marcellus fumed with anger and mortification, and was prepared to plunge still deeper into the course of violence and illegality. He protested that he would not listen to the harangues of demagogues while ten armed legions were appearing across the Alps. He, too, would summon an armed champion to defend the commonwealth.

Pompeius falls sick at Naples.
U.C. 704. B.C. 50.

But Pompeius meanwhile remained sluggish and inactive, and held aloof from these high-handed proceedings. He absented himself from the city, travelled from villa to villa, went to meet Cicero at Tarentum on his return from Cilicia; and the two veteran statesmen entertained one another with discourse on the position of affairs, which established some mutual confidence between them. Pompeius was suffering in bodily health, which no doubt prostrated his energies at this critical moment. His friends and allies were equally wondering at the eclipse which he had allowed to creep over him. But it was soon widely bruited that the great man had fallen sick of a fever at Neapolis, and was lying at the point of death. The report of his danger roused the sympathy of the Italians, which spread from city to city. The temples were crowded with devotees, sacrifices were offered, and vows recorded for his recovery. It was a singular instance of the vehemence of popular enthusiasm. When his health was unexpectedly restored, the people rushed tumultuously to congratulate their ancient favorite, and showered their blessings upon him as he was slowly transported in his litter to Rome. Memorable, indeed, was the example thus presented of the short-sightedness of mortals and the vanity of human wishes. The gods exclaimed the Roman moralists, offered, in their divine prescience, to remove the great Pompeius, at the summit of his fortunes, beyond the sphere of human contingencies; but the cities and the nations interposed with prayer, and preserved their beloved hero for defeat and decapitation. Pompeius himself was no less blind than his admirers. Estimating the depth of his influence by the loudness of these flattering acclamations, he no longer mistrusted the extent of his resources, nor doubted the terror of his name. There was no one at his ear to whisper to him how hollow these demonstrations were; to foretell that his garrisons would lay down their arms and Italy surrender without a blow, while the voices now most eager in their devotion to him would welcome the conqueror of Gaul with no less fervent enthusiasm. "But what," murmured Cicero, when the delusion was over, and his chief was shifting the basis of his power to a foreign shore, "what are the prospects of a party whose champion falls dangerously sick at least once a year?"

Cæsar's demands.

The Gallic legions, indeed, were still retained in their cantonments beyond the mountains; but the proconsul himself was drawing nearer to Rome, and the progress he now made through the cities of the Cisalpine, but strictly within the limits of his province, was a continued triumph and defiance. Under pretence of courting the suffrages of the citizens in that district for his quæstor Antonius, who was suing for the augurate, he passed the summer on the confines of his government. The people came to greet him on every side, or celebrated his arrival in their towns with feasts and sacrifices. From the Cisalpine he hastened back in the autumn to the country of the Treviri, where he had summoned his forces to a general review; and there he doubtless communicated to his officers his resolve to extort from the senate full satisfaction of all their demands—the consulship for himself, the honor of the triumph, and confirmation of the acts of his long proconsulship, with lands and money for his soldiers. "They cabal," he said, "to wrest from me my rights; but"—laying his hand on his sword—"this shall maintain them." At this moment Cicero had just returned from Cilicia, and sued for a triumph. Trifling as his successes had been, the greatest of all military honors had sometimes no doubt been granted for less. It was not a time for mortifying even the vanity of a good citizen. But Cato opposed himself to the demand with his surly impracticability, and the senate weakly or spitefully sanctioned the refusal. Pompeius, to whom Cicero had applied for his support, had amused his petitioner with hollow compliments, while Cæsar on his part expressed his warm approbation, together with the offer of his services, thus easily detaching him from the counsels of his ungenerous party, and disposing him to remain a mute spectator of the rapid advance of the crisis before him.

Vacillation of the senate.

The senate, meanwhile, made no actual preparation for the approaching contest. If Marcellus applied to Pompeius, and urged him to concentrate the legions which he had under his command in the West, he was satisfied, or at least silenced, with the great captain's vainglorious reply: "I have only to stamp with my foot, to raise up legions from the soil of Italy." Pompeius depended on the veterans to whom he had himself given lands, and to the sons, perhaps, of the veterans of Sulla. Neither he nor his adherents knew how slight was the tie which bound these graceless clients to him. The senators were reassured, however, by his boastful confidence, and, voting again at the bidding of their favorite consul, decided by a great majority, in the teeth of their recent vote, that Cæsar should be at once recalled and his rival be allowed at the same time to retain his powers. The injustice of this decision was palpable; nor less so that Cæsar, by yielding to it, would have rushed on his own destruction. It was impossible for him to come to the city, and sue for the consulship as a candidate in the toga. His life would not have been safe for a moment. Nor was it more safe for him even to descend into private life, and surrender his claim to the office which was necessary for his personal security. Once more Curio exclaimed against the action of the nobles, and the populace, perceiving the situation at a glance, hailed his efforts with tumultuous applause. The senate was alarmed, and swayed back again with the natural levity of the southern temperament. On a second division the consul was outvoted by a majority as great as that which had but just now supported him. Marcellus was baffled. He dismissed the senate, exclaiming, in his irritation: "You have carried the day, but you shall have Cæsar for your master."

Curio urges Cæsar to decisive action.

A few days later, at the commencement of December, the city was alarmed by a report that Cæsar's legions were crossing the Alps. The consuls hastily called the senate together, and proposed to summon some cohorts stationed at Capua to the defence of the city. Curio derided their fears, asserting that the rumor was untrue. It was at least premature. But Marcellus retorted that, prevented as he was from concerting with the supreme council for the safety of the state, he would venture to save it by measures of his own. He marched solemnly through the city, attended by the chiefs of his party, and sought Pompeius in his residence at Alba. There he thrust a sword into the imperator's hand, and invited him to assume the command of all the forces of the common wealth then in Italy. Pompeius accepted the charge, adding, with the pretended moderation which never for sook him, "If no better expedient can be discovered." He declined however to make further levies; he refused to recall the legions in the East or the West to the centre of the empire. He was either singularly careless or he still looked to an overt attack on the part of Cæsar to justify his assumption of extraordinary powers. The Gallic proconsul had now again quitted the Transalpine province and stationed himself at Ravenna. He was attended there by a single legion only, but other battalions were no doubt moving quietly southwards to its support. Yet it was hard to believe that he meditated any sudden outbreak, and possibly Marcellus was himself deceived by the vigor of his own stroke. Curio, however, who was more in his patron's secrets, pretended that the inviolability of his own person was no longer secure. Protesting against the consul's call to arms, and proclaiming that the reign of law was at an end, he suddenly quitted the city still early in December, and betook himself to the proconsul's quarters. The people regarded both the one and the other as victims of oligarchical injustice. The political atmosphere was fully charged with electricity. Curio was urgent for action. Cæsar still kept his head, waiting and watching for the fit moment with the arrival of the new year. Q. Cassius and M. Antonius, two of his most devoted officers, would succeed to the office of tribune; another Caius Marcellus, not less violent than the first, and Lentulus Crus, an uncompromising optimate, would become consuls a final collision would inevitably follow. He determined that the act of his own hand which should furnish direct occasion for it should be specious and popular. He commanded Curio to return and lay before the senate and people his offer to surrender at once the Transalpine province, together with the troops which held it, now ten months before the legal expiration of his office, retaining only the Cisalpine and Illyricum with the moderate force of two legions. Should these concessions be rejected, he would still be content to lay down his command without reserve, provided that Pompeius, on his part, should do the like. Failing the acceptance of this last condition, he boldly declared that he would come in arms to Rome, and avenge his own and what he affirmed to be his country's injuries.

The tribunes flee to Cæsar's camp.
U.C. 705. B.C. 49.

The letter containing these proposals was presented to the senate and the new consuls on the first day of the new year (B.C. 49) The bearer was refused even a hearing; but Cassius and Antonius took care that the people should be informed of them, and insisted that Cæsar's claims should be considered. A noisy and confused debate ensued. The consuls declared "the state in danger," and refused all concession to a "rebel with arms in his hands;" the senate ultimately adopted the motion of Scipio, that unless Cæsar yielded both army and province before a certain day, he should be treated as a public enemy. The tribunes interposed their vetos, exclaiming that the people had granted and prolonged his office, the people alone could legally with draw it. But no heed was paid to the voice of law or the forms of the constitution. The decree was carried by a large majority; the tribunes formally protesting, and declaring that they were coerced in the exercise of their legitimate functions. Their opponents retorted by a solemn proclamation of the danger of the state, and by inviting the citizens to put on mourning. Pompeius from his station outside the walls sent some cohorts into the city. The consuls were emboldened to act with a high hand. They convened the senate on the 6th of January to determine on the punishment of the refractory tribunes. When it was intimated to these officials that they would be formally expelled from the assembly, they pretended to disguise themselves and fled along with Curio, as if for their lives. In thus leaving the city they signified that they threw up their outraged and de fenceless office; for the tribune was forbidden to step outside the walls during his term of service. They were eagerly received in the proconsul's quarters. Cæsar could now take up their cause as his own, and the use of force would be doubly justified in the eyes of the people, ever sensitive of the privileges of their traditional protectors.

Cæsar appeals to arms.

Cæsar had suffered a technical wrong, and so had the tribunes also. Neither of them had perhaps any constitutional means of redress. Such illegal acts as those of the consuls and senate betrayed a signal defect in the Roman polity for which no legitimate remedy had been appointed, for which none, perhaps, was ultimately possible. Aggrieved as they doubtless were, were they morally justified in making an appeal to force? Such is the question which their countrymen asked themselves, both then and afterwards; but they could find no satisfactory answer. Such, again, is the question which the moderns have repeatedly asked, and again with no result. The problem is one which has had a deep interest for succeeding generations; for the consequences of Cæsar's bold resolve to vindicate his claims by arms have had a wide effect upon human history which has not even yet ceased to operate. Sulla and Marius and many other public men at Rome had acted with equal or greater violence, and no one has cared to inquire how far their circumstances excused or justified them; but all the world has taken a common interest in criticising the action of the immortal Cæsar.

Lucan's estimate of the causes of the civil war.—Division of sovereignty among three rulers.—Rivalry of Pompeius and Cæsar.

A full century later, when passions, it may be supposed, had cooled, and the conditions of the problem admitted of calmer consideration, the poet Lucan gives us the final judgment of his own contemporaries. Lucan was a poet, but he had sat at the feet of statesmen and philosophers; he was an ardent enthusiast for liberty, but his notions of liberty were those of a Roman oligarch and the heir of senatorial prejudices. The first sentence of his poem paradoxically characterizes the civil war as a justifiable outrage—"Jus datum sceleri;" and waiving all subtle technical criticism on the merits of the case, he refers it to a moral necessity, such as places it altogether beyond the scope of human judgment. The doctrine of the Stoics, which he had imbibed from his uncle Seneca, assured him that all mundane things are subject to a natural law of production and decay; and that as the frame of the universe itself is doomed to return to Chaos, so the noblest creations of human genius must run their destined course, and finally crumble to their foundations. "In se magna ruunt:" Great things fall by their own bulk and greatness. The commonwealth of Rome had reached the summit of its triumphs, and straightway Fate stepped in and claimed her victim. Nevertheless, within the controlling action of this primal law there is room, he allows, for secondary causes. The immediate impulse to revolution was given, he says, by the division of political power between the three conspiring chiefs, and the exclusion of the people from the direction of their own affairs. This tyranny, disguised by its partition among three equals, must eventually centre in one alone; for such colleagues cannot fail to become rivals, and such rivals must at last rush in arms against each other. So had even the rising walls of Rome been moistened with a brother's blood. Crassus indeed, while he yet lived, had stood, like a slender isthmus, between encroaching oceans; on his death no barrier remained to part the contending claims of Cæsar and Pompeius. Julia carried to her early grave the last bond of union between two alien houses; she who like the Sabine women of ancient legend, might have flung herself between the husband and the father, and dashed away their swords and joined their hands together. Thenceforth there was only jealousy on the one side and ambition on the other; Pompeius could not brook an equal nor Cæsar a superior. Betwixt them who should decide the right? The gods pronounced in favor of the victor, but Cato had concurred with the vanquished. But the contending champions came into the field on no equal terms. The one was old in years and content with the applause of the forum and the theatre; the other ardent and active, flushed with recent victories, and eager for power; the one had long adopted the garb of peace the other had not yet sheathed the sword which had subdued the Gauls. Pompeius stood like the veteran oak, conspicuous and alone in some fertile field, crowned with the trophies of many triumphs, majestic in its decay, and revered for its ancient associations. Cæsar fell upon it like the lightning of Jupiter, which spares nothing venerable, nothing holy, neither the monarch of the forest nor the temples of its own divinity.

Luxury and vices of the times.

Such, he continues, were the causes of enmity between the illustrious rivals; but the seeds of discord lay far deeper, and pervaded the commonwealth itself with the fatal germs of dissolution. Luxury, and the wealth of cities and empires amassed in a few hands, had transformed the equal Citizens of Rome into a group of rival tyrants who cajoled or trampled upon a herd of paupers. The thirst of gold and the ruthless means by which it had been gratified, had blunted all sense of public or private honor. No eminence satisfied the ambitious aspirant but one which towered above the laws; no power contented him but such as defied the commonwealth itself. The decrees of the senate, the resolutions of the people, were alike coerced or disregarded. Consuls and tribunes vied with one another in violating the restrictions imposed on them by the laws. Every honor was bought with money or extorted by force; the citizens set their own price on their favor, while the recurring elections of the Field of Mars brought the republic year by year to the verge of anarchy and dissolution. The men most powerful in the camp, most influential in the comitia, were plunged in the deepest embarrassments, from which war alone could extricate them; the usurers, the last element of national stability, trembled for their preposterous ventures, while spendthrifts and bankrupts invoked with all their vows the chances of universal confusion.

Monarchy a consummation plainly inevitable.

Such is the view which Lucan took—such are nearly the words in which he explained it—of the causes of the great civil war. His compliment to the despotism of Nero, as the sole means of restoring order, may be suspected of hypocrisy and adulation. Nevertheless, the fact is indisputable, that everything had been long tending to monarchy, and that for the last eighty years the decay of ancient ideas, the obliteration of republican manners, and the disorganization of government, had combined to render such a consummation inevitable. The tribunate of the younger Gracchus, the consulships of Marius and Cinna, the dictatorship of Sulla, the wide and protracted commands of Pompeius and Cæsar, had been in fact no other than temporary autocracies. The nobles were content that the state should be ruled by a series of extraordinary commissions of their own appointment; the people would have willingly merged all their rights of self-government in the paramount authority of a sovereign pledged to subject the nobles to them. The readers and thinkers of the day, a small but increasing class, withdrew more and more from the turbid sphere of political action. Atticus, who piqued himself on his practical shrewdness, professed neutrality on all questions of state, and lived in amity with three generations of public men of every faction. Cato and his nephew Brutus, who strove to mould their public conduct by the precepts of the highest philosophy, only proved that virtue and honor could no longer live untainted in the atmosphere of the Roman free-state. The republic to which Cicero devoted his faith and love was the republic of antiquity, the republic of his own imagination, the republic of the good and wise; nor are indications wanting that even he admitted that liberty is never more amiable than when she yields to the mild authority of a constitutional sovereign. But few men were cautious and temperate as he was; the bold and freespoken openly proclaimed, with Curio, that "the republic was a vain chimera;" or called it, with Cæsar himself, "a mere name devoid of substance or reality."

Sentiments conveyed in "Sallust's letters to Cæsar."

The fact of such a movement of men's spirits in the direction of royalty is one of the great lessons we learn from the history of the Roman commonwealth; the history of a vigorous nation governed by a close aristocracy of birth, which asserted for itself the full power and privileges of government, and slowly and with reluctance conceded a share in them to the popular class below it. The people were driven, by want and jealousy, to support the ambition of any one among the ruling class who would take them and their interests under his protection. Their minds became gradually prepared for the abandonment of their personal freedom; all the specious arguments in favor of monarchy obtained more and more a hearing with them, and writers or speakers soon arose who could place them in a light sufficiently effective. Such a writer is one whose "Letters addressed to Cæsar" go under the name of Sallust the historian. This tract does not indeed deserve to be considered genuine; but it seems to belong at least to the period before us, and to speak the common sentiments of the public men of the day who despaired of the free-state. In these letters Cæsar is invited to assume the government, as the only man who can heal the public disorders. "Save Rome," exclaims the orator, "for, if Rome perishes, the world will perish with her in blood and ruin. Vast is the task imposed upon you. The genuine free people is annihilated; there remains only a corrupt populace without unity of sentiment or action. Infuse a new element into the mass; introduce numbers of foreign citizens; found colonies and restore cities; crush the faction of tyrants at home, and extend far the roots of the Roman community abroad. Exact military service of all alike (not of Romans or Latins only), but limit the term of it. Let the magistrates be chosen for their virtues, not merely for their riches. To entrust to the citizens themselves the working of this reformed polity would be useless. But the impartial eye of a sovereign ruler may watch securely over it, and neither fear, nor favor, nor interest must he suffered to impede its operation." This exposition of the views of intelligent public men was supported by the mass of the middle classes; it was sanctioned by many from disgust at the corruption of the optimates. Nevertheless, the ruling powers would doubtless struggle for their ascendency. The revolution in view must be a work of force and of manifold perils. The atrocities of Sulla had not been forgotten. Again and again the nobles would surely resort to violence and bloodshed. Even at this moment it was reported that the government had prepared a list of forty senators, and multitudes of lesser quality, for proscription. But Cæsar had already gained a name for personal clemency, and his success was anticipated as a pledge of public and private security.

Cæsar's pretensions regarded with favor by provincials, subjects, and foreigners.

The sentiment in favor of Cæsar's aggression received, no doubt, further impulse from the partiality of the provincials. To the foreign subjects of the republic monarchy was, for the most part, more familiar than the forms of a commonwealth; and to the multitudes of Greeks and Asiatics who thronged the streets of Rome the populace lent an attentive ear when they dilated on the pomp and splendour of Oriental royalty. But Cæsar himself was personally beloved by the very people whom he had conquered, as well as by multitudes who had never seen him. The nephew of Marius had carried the traditions of his party further than any of his predecessors. The incorporation of the Italians was not enough for him. He had advanced the Cispadane Gauls to the franchise also; he was evidently prepared to carry the same policy onward. The Gauls beyond the Po, and even beyond the Alps, might expect similar favor at his hands. He had secured the independence of certain communities in Greece. He had attached to himself some of the potentates of Asia. The whole nation of the Jews, very popular at this period in Rome, loved him as much as they hated his opponent. Cæsar had lavished vast sums in the decoration of provincial cities, both in the East and West. Foreign nations might well imagine that the conqueror and organizer of Gaul was preparing to mould the whole Roman world into a mighty monarchy under equal laws. To be a second Alexander had been the dream of many kings and conquerors. The hour and the man might seem to have at last arrived for its realization.

Cæsar on his return to Italy.

"Would that I had seen," exclaims the French historian Michelet, "that man of pale and sallow countenance, faded before its time by the dissipations of the city, the delicate and epileptic Cæsar, marching at the head of his legions beneath the rainy skies of Gaul, swimming across our Gaulish rivers, or riding on horseback between the litters which bore his exhausted secretaries, dictating four or six letters at a time (seven, says Pliny, when he had no other business in hand), agitating Rome from the depths of Belgium, exterminating on his way two millions of enemies, subduing in ten years the Continent to the Rhine and the Northern Ocean." Such was the Cæsar who had quitted the city for his province; such had been his career during his long but voluntary exile; and now at last he was returning: his conquests completed, his dangers overcome, his bodily vigor strengthened, no doubt, by the toils he had endured; his mental powers strained to the utmost, his fame established, his character purged in the eyes of his countrymen by merits and sufferings, all Rome prepared to bow before the genius which was now shining forth and eclipsing the long-faded glories of every other candidate for their worship. Cæsar exerted a moral and intellectual force which kindled to flame the imagination of his countrymen. Great as he was, transcendently great among the leaders of the people, great as a speaker, great as a writer, great as a statesman, greatest of all as a military chieftain, the excitable temperament of the Romans was already prone to adore him as greater than he was or ever could be.

CHAPTER VII.
(U.C. 705. B.C. 50.—U.C. 708. B.C. 46.)

THE CIVIL WAR.—BATTLE OF PHARSALIA.—DEATH OF POMPEIUS.—DEATH OF CATO.

Preparations of Pompeius and the consuls.—Cæsar crosses the Rubicon.

THE tribunes had quitted the city on the night of January 6 (=Nov. 13, B.C. 50, before the revision of the calendar). The consuls thereupon convoked the senate in the temple of Bellona, which lay outside the walls, in order to enable Pompeius to attend their meeting and virtually to control it. Their favored leader had attained the object of his ambition; the republic had thrown itself at his feet. New levies were commanded throughout Italy. Favonius petulantly urged him to "stamp with his foot," and evoke armed legions from the soil. But the wary veteran determined to leave in Spain the large forces which he had collected in his province, to act as a check upon Cæsar in his rear. Both he and the chiefs of his party still clung to the idea that their foe would be betrayed by disaffection in his own ranks. They were aware, perhaps, that his lieutenant Labienus was about to desert him, and they hoped that many others would follow his example. They were still convinced that the clouds of danger would disperse, and assigned magistracies and provinces among themselves and their adherents with reckless disregard even of the due forms of law. But Pompeius continued to make preparations for a lengthened conflict. Arms and money were collected by forced contributions; Italy was placed under military perquisition; her temples were rifled of their treasures. The report of these tumultuary proceedings reached Cæsar at Ravenna, where his plans were already matured. He harangued the soldiers of the single legion which he had there with him, explained his wrongs to the full satisfaction of their blunt understandings, and called upon them to draw their swords and hasten to redress them. On the morning of the 15th he sent forward some cohorts to the Rubicon, the frontier stream of his province. Throughout the day he presented himself at a public spectacle, invited company to his table, and entertained them with his usual affability. At sunset he made an excuse for a brief absence, and hastened with a few attendants to overtake his soldiers. The Romans signalized the famous passage of the Rubicon with various reputed marvels; but the act which decided the fate of Rome for so many centuries was quickly and quietly accomplished. On the morrow the proconsul of Gaul appeared in arms before Ariminum, as an invader of Italy. The Gauls were marching upon Rome; the frontier garrison opened its gates in terror. It was here that the tribunes met him in their flight from Rome; but what should have detained them ten days on their journey does not clearly appear. From these quarters Cæsar issued his orders for the movement of his troops; one legion reached him within a fortnight, another in the course of the next month. For the moment, however, his whole force was hardly six thousand strong, while his opponents had at least three times that number actually in hand. But Pompeius, it seemed, was struck with consternation, together with all his party, at these rapid movements. They were, after all, taken by surprise and utterly unmanned. The proscriptions of Marius, the slaughter of the Allia, the burning of the city by the Gauls, such were the horrors that seized on their imaginations, and unnerved them for the encounter.

Pompeius retires from Rome.

Pompeius betook himself to the Appian Way, and magistrates and nobles streamed through the gates and pressed after him to the southward. His forces, he declared, were unequal to the contest; let all good citizens follow him to a place of security. At Capua he halted, and there it was found that the consuls had carried away the keys of the temple of Saturn, but had left the treasure of the state behind them. Pompeius bade them fly back and fetch it; but they hesitated and asked for an escort. He could not spare a man. The gladiators in keeping at Capua required a large force to watch them. It was not till these dangerous swordsmen were broken up into small parties and lodged in security that the two legions which kept guard over them could be utilized for more active service.

The cities of central Italy surrender to Cæsar.

Meanwhile there was some pretence at negotiation; but Pompeius, encouraged by the defection of Labienus, insisted that Cæsar should lay down his arms, while Cæsar no less peremptorily demanded that if one surrendered his command the other should do so likewise. But Cæsar advanced; Arretium, Iguvium, and Auximum promptly received him. The road to Rome lay open to him; but when he heard that his adversaries were crossing from Capua to the Upper Coast, he turned to the left and threw himself on the strong central position of Corfinium, where Pompeius had left a detachment to hold him in check. Domitius Ahenobarbus, one of the boldest and most sanguine of the party, had insisted that this place at least should not be abandoned; but to leave it unsupported was equivalent to abandoning it. Domitius preferred to stand a siege, but his soldiers delivered up the place to the assailant as soon as he appeared before it. Domitius himself fell into the victor's hands; but Cæsar well knew the advantage of making a signal example of clemency, and not only spared the captive's life, but allowed him his freedom also. Politic as Cæsar's forbearance was, it accorded, doubtless, with his natural temper. Barbarous as he had shown himself in contest with the enemies of the state, he was always sparing of the blood of the citizens. He could be not forbearing only, but generous.

Pompeius makes his escape from Italy.

The beaten soldiers joined his standard with alacrity; the people of the country flocked around him. They were dismayed by the proclamations of Pompeius, who threatened the severest measures against all who assisted or countenanced his enemy. Cicero, who was deeply mortified at his chief's abandonment of the city, murmured with disgust at these impolitic menaces. Pompeius charged him to relinquish Capua, where he had been entrusted with a command, and join him in Apulia. He was loth to withdraw further from the city; and the road, it seems, was no longer open. From Luceria

Pompeius led the consuls and magistrates to the port of Brundisium. There he had already secured a number of transports, and from thence he immediately despatched several legions to Epirus. To remain himself behind and embark with the last of his division, was the only duty of a general that he consented to perform. Cæsar, hastening from Corfinium, was already at the gates; but he was destitute of vessels, and the sea was open to the transports, which were returning to bear away the remnant of the fugitives. He made a vigorous attempt to throw a mole across the mouth of the harbor but in this operation he was baffled, and Pompeius effected his escape.

Pompeius throws himself on his resources in the East.

The situation was now completely reversed. Pompeius and Cæsar had exchanged places. The government of Rome had emigrated to a foreign shore; the assailant reigned supreme throughout Italy, and had only to show himself in the city to be received with acclamations. The senators, at the bidding of their champion, had thrown themselves upon the support of subjects or strangers. While still possessed of large armies and abundant resources in the West, they had preferred to secure their position in the opposite quarter of the empire. They carried with them all the levies which they had made from Roman citizens, with several complete legions, and were accompanied by the great mass of the ruling classes, the knights and publicani, whose pecuniary interests were bound up with lands and cities in the Eastern provinces; and they demanded aid from all the dependent sovereigns who lined the frontiers of Greece and Asia Minor, the petty kings of Thrace, of Galatia, of Cappadocia, and others, who could furnish ample military supplies, as well as dense crowds of well-equipped though ill trained warriors. They were protected, moreover, from any sudden attack by a numerous fleet, which, after transporting them across the Adriatic, could guard the passage against the assailant, should he threaten to pursue them. Cæsar himself was utterly unprovided with ships or maritime resources. The great naval powers of the Mediterranean, Rhodes, and Egypt, were attached by special bonds to the interests of Pompeius. He had not calculated on having to pursue the senate on the ocean.

Cæsar repairs to Rome.

Nevertheless, the moral weight lay on the side of Cæsar, and this soon appeared to be preponderant. The flight of Pompeius was viewed with disgust and alarm by a large section of his own supporters. Cato took the same step only as a frightful necessity. Cicero shrank from it, and returned to Rome to abide the progress of events. Many senators and other men of consequence followed his example. Public men and magnates who possessed a stake in the country were terrified at the violent language of the fugitives, who threatened to return as conquerors and tyrants. Pompeius was wont to exclaim: "Sulla could do this and that; why should not I?" Sulla had brought his legions from the East, and made himself dictator by massacre. His pupil and successor might do the like. Confiscation, plunder, and proscription were in the mouths of his most rabid followers, such as Bibulus, Favonius, Labienus, and Lentulus. Nor was the state of things secure at Rome itself. The government was dissolved; the consuls and higher magistrates had fled from the forum; the laws were in abeyance, and a reign of anarchy seemed impending. The domestic warfare of the debtors and creditors, which had so often brought the republic to the verge of ruin, which had been arrested by the overthrow of Catilina, and with difficulty kept under by the authority and the armed forces of Pompeius, was about to blaze out again. Every day of the interregnum was fraught with infinite peril. Cæsar was not in a position to pursue Pompeius; but had he been so, it would have been necessary for him to abandon the pursuit till he had secured the basis of his power at home. He had driven his enemies out of Italy in sixty days; he now turned promptly back, crossed the Apennines, and presented himself, almost unattended, in the city. The people high and low received him joyfully, for he brought them the pledge of security at least for the day, and they had almost ceased, through their long period of anxiety and despair, to look forward to the morrow.

Cæsar seizes the treasure in the temple of Saturn.

Thus possessed of the centre of his enemies' position, the conqueror might determine more at leisure on which wing of their forces he should first throw himself. In the absence of the civil magistrates, he could only impose a military government on the city; but this was cheerfully accepted. A large donative gratified his soldiers; a liberal gratuity to every citizen delighted the populace. But he carefully abstained from private spoliation for the discharge of these sums. He bethought himself of the treasure which the consuls had forgotten to carry away, and ordered the temple of Saturn to be thrown open to him. L. Metellus, one of the tribunes, was on the spot, and had the courage to interpose his inviolable person. Cæsar pushed him scornfully aside; he addressed the people, reminding them that the precious store was reserved as a sacred deposit for repelling a Gallic invasion. It was believed to comprise the actual ingots of gold which Rome had paid to Brennus as the ransom of the city, and which Camillus had wrested again from the barbarians at the point of the sword. "No fear henceforth," he cried, "of a Gallic invasion: I have subdued the Gauls."

Curio is slain in Africa.

But the Pompeian party had yet another weapon in store which might make the position of their adversary untenable. The nearest granaries of the city, Sardinia, Sicily, and Africa, were all held at the moment by their own officers, while Egypt itself was very closely connected with their chief and his interests. Cæsar's first care now was to establish his power in the neighboring islands. A legion which be promptly despatched to Sardinia was received by the inhabitants with open arms, while the garrison of the senate was ignominiously expelled from it. Cato, who had charge of Sicily, was obliged to abandon his post as soon as Curio appeared in sight. Africa still remained to conquer; but Curio, when he transported his forces to the continent, was encountered by the Pompeian lieutenant Varus, with the Numidian chieftain Juba at his side, and was routed and slain. This important province was thus left in the hands of the senate; but the immediate needs of the city were now adequately supplied.

Cæsar conquers the Pompeian forces in Spain.

Meanwhile Cæsar, having left Rome in the keeping of Æmilius Lepidus— a noble of high position, whose descent and connections attached him to his cause—and the Italian peninsula under the command of his devoted follower M. Antonius, had set off in person for Spain. "I go," he said, "to encounter an army without a general; I shall return to attack a general without an army." The three Iberian provinces were held by good and veteran soldiers; but were commanded by Varro, Afranius, and Petreius, a man of letters, a man of fashion, and a stiff regimental officer. Cæsar might hope to despatch them all quickly; but he was detained by the defection of Massilia, which lay on his route, and now shut its gates against him at the instigation of Domitius, the same Pompeian officer whom he had so recently spared at Corfinium. This important city held as it were the keys of the Transalpine province, of which it was the principal emporium. It was necessary to reduce it at any sacrifice of time and resources; but Cæsar left three legions to invest it, while he passed by it himself, and pushed on, crossing the Pyrenees, and throwing himself upon the Pompeian forces which held the line of the Ebro. The events of the brief and spirited campaign which followed are told in the concise and nervous narrative of the conqueror, who succeeded, after suffering great hardships from flood and famine, and displaying singular ability and fruitfulness of resource, in reducing his opponents to submission. The Pompeian soldiers for the most part took service under him; once more Afranius and Petreius, with their principal officers, were allowed to go free. From Ilerda Cæsar marched swiftly south ward, and easily brought Varro to terms at Corduba. There he found a store of treasure already accumulated for the campaign against him, and returned from his adventurous expedition reinforced with fresh supplies both of men and money. The Massilians made no further resistance. Domitius escaped and rejoined Pompeius in Epirus, and added another element of rashness and violence to his noisy and discordant camp. But Cæsar had effected the reduction of the West. At this moment he might have declared himself the acknowledged sovereign of one half of the empire.

Cæsar is created dictator.—Importance of his fiscal measures.

During his absence the citizens at Rome, inspired by his influential agent, Lepidus, had proclaimed him dictator. Some of the prescribed forms had indeed been omitted; but little care of legal forms had been taken in many recent elections. The dictator had been created, it seems, by the prætor, in place of the consul, with the acclamations of the people, and not by the suffrage of the senate or the curies. It was better, however, that the commander of the legions should rule under a known historical title than with none at all. The people, who saw the odious power of a dictator wielded at last by a champion of their own, rejoiced in the master whom they seemed to have themselves chosen, and forgot for the moment that Cæsar ruled by the army and not by the voice of their comitia. It was for fiscal measures which brooked neither delay nor weakness, that the appointment of a dictator was demanded at this crisis. When, in the middle of the seventh century of the city, the futile laws against usury had been suffered to fall into abeyance, a consul was found to carry a sweeping law for the reduction of all debts by three-fourths. The money-lenders, who demanded interest from twelve to forty per cent., exclaimed loudly against this confiscation of their property; but it was impossible to maintain the government except by such violent enactments from time to time. Nor indeed did the money-lenders of Rome suffer permanently from these arbitrary measures, any more than the Jews suffered from even harsher interference with their gains in the Middle Ages. The spirit of luxury growing with the greatness of the empire gave fresh impulse to their transactions. Large classes of citizens were lying overwhelmed by the weight of their obligations. Among the various interests evoked in favor of Cæsar's schemes, none were more attached to him than those of the debtors and repudiators. His hereditary connection with the party opposed to the noblest and wealthiest classes, his reputed familiarity with Catilina, his own early embarrassments and laxity of principles entailed by them, all pointed him out as the destined leader of a great fiscal revolution. But the anticipations thus formed of him were deceived. Assailed by clamorous importunity, the dictator, absolute as he was, refused to yield to the cry for confiscation. He appointed arbitrators for the valuation of debtors' property, and insisted on its sale; all he required of the creditors was that they should forego their claims for excessive interest. He seems, further, to have resorted to the old expedient of the tribunes in distributing grants of land among the bankrupts, and relieving the state from the dangers of a needy aristocracy.

Cæsar establishes regular government, and then abdicates.

The chief measures of Cæsar's dictatorship included a liberal distribution to the wants of the poorer citizens, the revocation of the enactments of Sulla which had condemned even the children of his victims to civil incapacity, and the concession of citizenship to the inhabitants of the Cisalpine. At the end of eleven days he abdicated his office; but be caused himself to be elected consul, together with his now declared adherent, Servilius, for the ensuing year. The actual consuls were suffered to retain their nominal magistracy to the close of their legitimate term, which was at the moment expiring. Nothing was henceforth wanting to the regularity of his government: neither the decrees of a senate—for he had assembled more than one-half of its members at Rome—nor the election of the people, nor the sanction of the curies and of the auspices taken on the spot appointed by religion. Cæsar, as proconsul, was a rebel from the moment he quitted his province; but as soon as he became consul, lawfully installed, the right seemed to pass at once to his side, while his adversaries were transformed into enemies and traitors. This they themselves tacitly acknowledged; for, numerous as they were, influential as they seemed to be, they dared not enact a law, nor hold an election, nor confer an imperium. The representative of the people had become the guardian of usage and public order, while the champion of the oligarchy derived his arbitrary power from the passions of a turbulent camp. But in fact the names both of Senate and People were little regarded amidst the excitement of personal contention. Cæsar and Pompeius were now the real watchwords of parties; and even the children playing in the streets divided themselves, we are told, into Cæsarians and Pompeians.

Cæsar crosses the Adriatic. U.C. 706. B.C. 48.—
Cæsar checked before Petra.

Cæsar, victorious everywhere by land, had made no effort, it would seem, to contest with his adversary the possession of the sea. He trusted to the rapidity of his movements and to the many chances of maritime enterprise, to throw his forces across the narrow channel between Italy and Epirus, and evade or discomfit the flotillas opposed to him. He reached Brundisium, where he had collected a number of transports, and on the 4th of January, B.C. 48, three days from his leaving Rome, he embarked seven legions, amounting to 15,000 infantry and 600 cavalry. Bibulus, the commander of the Pompeian fleet, failed to intercept them, and could only attack and destroy the empty vessels on their return to receive a second division. Cæsar had himself crossed over with the first, but he was not in a position to act with vigor until the arrival of Antonius with additional succors. He is said to have hastened, in his impatience, to bring over these reinforcements in person, and to have been driven back by a tempest in which he had with difficulty persuaded his trembling pilot to embark. "Fear not," he had exclaimed; "you carry Cæsar and his fortunes." When indeed Antonius succeeded at last in crossing, he was wafted a hundred miles below the point where his chief expected him; and Pompeius, who lay between, might easily, it should seem, have overpowered him. But most of the places on the coast had eagerly attached themselves to the cause of the assailant. The means of supply for the unwieldy hosts of the senate were not, perhaps, easily attainable. Whatever was the cause of this delay Cæsar promptly took advantage of it. He was enabled to throw himself between Pompeius and his magazines at Dyrrhachium, and confine him to his secure position on the rocky promontory of Petra. Pompeius indeed felt little concern at this manœuvre. He could occupy himself in training the loose and motley auxiliaries who had thronged to his standard, even while his adversary, with such inferior numbers, ventured to draw his lines around him. The confinement, however, of the great commander by his daring assailant could not fail to have a great moral effect, dispiriting his own friends and exalting the hopes and expectations of his enemies, and of the populations which watched them far and near. After a time Pompeius found his situation become intolerable; he made a strenuous and well-directed attack upon his besiegers, broke their lines with his superior force, and drove them from before him. But Cæsar had now secured a party in the heart of Greece and Macedonia, and thither he retreated, intending probably to fall upon Scipio, who was bringing succors to his son-in-law from the East. Pompeius hastened to follow him. The two rival captains dogged each other's steps from place to place, till at last they met in the valley of the Enipeus, an affluent of the Peneüs, on the plains of Pharsalia.

Both armies manœuvre in Thessaly.

The nobles in the senatorial camp had amused themselves with quarrelling about the expected spoils of the war, which they hoped to terminate with a triumphant victory. Cato was so shocked with their truculent threats that he sought a command which should detain him on the coast of Epirus; and Cicero, who had repaired once more to the side of Pompeius, now pleaded ill-health, and remained behind also. But the more sanguine spirits of the party still urged their chief to the battle from which he would fain have shrunk; nor could his officers bring him into the field till Cæsar threatened a flank movement which would have cut off his communications. Yet his army boasted a legionary force fully 40,000 strong, with 7,000 horse, supported by a countless host of foreign allies while Cæsar had but 22,000 well-trained infantry and 1,000 cavalry, with a few irregular battalions.

Battle of Pharsalia.
U.C. 706. B.C. 48.

On August 9 (June 6) the Pompeians descended from their camp to the plain beneath, having the little stream of the Enipeus on their right. Cæsar hastened to the encounter, levelling the ramparts of his entrenchments to facilitate the egress of his troops in line of battle. Extending his cavalry on his right, he ordered his first line to charge, after halting just before they came within reach of their opponents' spears, to take breath for the final onset. The knights and senators who fought in the Pompeian ranks were equipped in complete armor, and the Cæsarians were directed to waste no blows on their helms and corslets, but strike direct at their unprotected faces. Thus assailed, they soon broke their ranks, retreated, and fled, the support of the cavalry on their flanks having been baffled by Cæsar's German horse. Pompeius had already abandoned the field, retiring to his camp at the first turn of fortune. There he would have rallied his troops and defended the works, but the routed battalions fled precipitately past them. The Cæsarians pressed closely upon him, and almost surprised him in his tent. Leaping on his horse at the last moment, he galloped swiftly away, escaped through the hinder gate, nor drew rein till he had reached Larissa. His discomfited battalions made a faint show of defence at a good position which they had assumed in the rear of their encampment; but, dismayed by the flight of their commander, they soon gave way before the renewed attack of their indefatigable pursuers. It was Cæsar's maxim to "think nothing done while aught remained to do;" and on this occasion he exemplified it to the utmost. He allowed his victorious soldiers no respite till the whole force of the Pompeians was utterly dispersed, or reduced to capitulate before nightfall. A few only of the senators got away in the darkness.

The loss on both sides.

The battle of Pharsalia obtained, however, one honorable distinction in the annals of civil warfare. From the close of the day no more blood was shed; the fugitives were spared, and the captives received mercy. The victors lost only thirty centurions and two hundred, or, as some stated, twelve hundred legionaries; of the vanquished there fell ten senators, forty knights, and six thousand of all ranks of citizens. The slaughter among the foreign auxiliaries was probably much greater. Domitius was the only noble of distinction that perished; he was cut down in the flight by Cæsar's cavalry. Many were captured; many also hastened to give themselves up to the conqueror, whose fame for clemency was now generally established. As he rode across the field of battle he expressed his grief, and perhaps his remorse, at the sight of his countrymen's corpses. "They would have it so," he exclaimed; "after all my exploits I should have been lost had I not thrown myself on the protection of my soldiers." Assuredly this was true enough, whatever he the value of the excuse.

Pompeius seeks refuge in Egypt, and is there murdered.

The remnant of the vast army of the East was scattered far and wide. No reserve had been provided on the field, no place assigned for rallying at a distance. Even the naval force was dispersed or distant. Pompeius rushed through Larissa, hurried down the vale of Tempe to the mouth of the Peneüs, took ship on board a merchant vessel with a handful of attendants, and gained the island of Lesbos, whither he had removed his wife Cornelia. Running thence along the coast of Asia, he picked up a few of his adherents, and held council with them, chiefly, it would seem, about his own personal safety. His first idea of seeking an asylum at the court of Parthia was indignantly overruled. To take refuge with the king of Egypt, a dependent of the republic, was deemed both safer and less dishonorable. The wealth of Egypt was unbounded, its position well-nigh inaccessible to an enemy destitute of a fleet. Ptolemæus was young and, doubtless, timid; possibly he might acknowledge a duty towards the senate which had befriended him. Pompeius arrived off Pelusium with about 2,000 men—too few or too many for his safety. The court of Alexandria had well weighed the situation. Engaged as it was in a contest with Cleopatra, the king's sister, it discussed the claims of the Roman fugitive, but rejected his dangerous alliance. The victim was inveigled into a boat, under pretence of being conveyed into the royal presence. He was murdered at a blow, and his head cut off to be presented to Cæsar on his expected arrival. The body was flung into the surf, where it was picked up by a charitable hand, and hastily consumed with fuel from a broken vessel. On the stone which covered the remains the same hand inscribed with a blackened brand the illustrious name of "Magnus." The history of Rome, fertile as it is in tragic issues, affords no more signal instance of a reverse of political fortune. But though Pompeius must fill, next to Cæsar, the largest space on our canvas, his character was common and uninteresting, and his career, however splendid and dramatic, has left no such impress on the history of the times as that of his great rival, or even that of Cicero or of Cato.

Cæsar establishes himself at Alexandria.
U.C. 706-7.

Pompeius had fled from the scene of his defeat; but the sea was closed against the conqueror by his naval armaments. Cæsar was enabled, indeed, by the treachery of C. Cassius, who commanded in the straits, to throw himself across the Hellespont; but though the military forces of the senate had dispersed in all directions, and offered no resistance, he could not transport his own army into Asia, but was attended in his pursuit of Pompeius by no more than a single legion. In the Asiatic provinces, however, he was received with enthusiasm, and forwarded on his way. Pompeius had gained no love throughout the ample regions he had conquered and organized. Cæsar picked up a few vessels on the coast, and presented himself, with four thousand men, before the capital of the Ptolemies within a few days from the death of his rival. The king's ministers hastened to produce the head of the murdered man; but he turned from it with horror. Without a moment's delay or hesitation, he entered Alexandria in military array, with the ensigns of a Roman imperator and consul. The populace was disturbed. Mercenary battalions, composed of Greeks, Romans, and Asiatics, which maintained the unpopular throne of the Macedonian dynasty, were excited to quarrel with the Cæsarians, and some encounters took place between them. Cæsar required money. He seized on the person of the young king; he listened to the solicitations of the king's sister, Cleopatra, who was intriguing against her brother, and required him to share his power with her. But the king's ministers, who had offended her, trembled for themselves. One of them, Pothinus, was arrested and put to death; but Achillas called the soldiers and citizens to arms, enclosed the intruding Roman in one quarter of the city, and reduced him to desperate straits, in the crisis of which he was obliged to swim for his life, with his Commentaries, so said the legend, in one hand. In the course of his defence Cæsar fired the Egyptian fleet, and the flames consumed the great library of the museum, with its 400,000 volumes. He consented at last to restore Ptolemæus; but on the arrival of reinforcements from Syria he was enabled to assume the offensive. He overthrew the royal army on the banks of the Nile, when Ptolemæus himself perished in the stream. The Egyptians accepted Cleopatra for their queen at the command of the conqueror.

Campaign against Pharnaces.
U.C. 707. B.C. 47,

We can hardly suppose that the great warrior and statesman allowed himself to be drawn into this perilous adventure by the charm, as has been commonly reported, of Cleopatra's beauty and accomplishments. More probably he had we fixed his eye on the treasures of Alexandria, the wealthiest city of the ancient world, to furnish him with the means he so much required, while he firmly abstained from the usual resource of plunder and confiscation.

When at last his fortune extricated him from the struggle, he allowed himself indeed to remain three months longer to complete the advantage he had gained. As long as the Pompeians were still scattered, he lost little by postponing the prosecution of the war against them. He might even wish the disheartened remnant to gather head again, that he might once more strike them down at a blow. Meanwhile, he made a campaign against Pharnaces, the son of Mithridates, who had profited by the general confusion to attack Deiotarus and Ariobarzanes. These Eastern kings had been enrolled as allies of Pompeius, but they were dependents of the republic also, and as such Cæsar now undertook to defend them. Again, perhaps, he was in want of money. The assailant was easily defeated in the battle of Zela; so speedily indeed that the victor, according to the story, could announce his success to the senate in the three words *Vent, vidi, vici,*—"I came, I saw, I conquered." After regulating with all despatch the affairs of the East, he hastened back to Italy, where his presence began to be required.

Disturbances in Italy.
U.C. 707.

The measures which the dictator had enacted for the adjustment of debts could not be universally acceptable. Many other causes of discontent were rife in the city and throughout Italy. Cælius, a clever intriguer, who, like Curio before him, had deceived even Cicero by his pretensions to patriotism, excited disturbance at Rome. The consul Servilius acted with firmness, and caused him to be expelled from the senate and declared incapable of public office. Thereupon he joined himself with Milo, who had crept out of his place of banishment and had armed his numerous gladiators in the south of Italy; and the two together raised a tumultuary force of outlaws and banditti. The sedition, however, was promptly suppressed, and both its leaders perished.

Cæsar dictator a second time.
U.C. 707. B.C. 47.

It required a strong hand to maintain a secure and settled government amidst the perils which threatened it from within and from without.

Doubtless, the attachment of the citizens to Cæsar was confirmed by the ferocious menaces of the Pompeians, which still reached them from a distance. Even the victory of Pharsalia could hardly avail to reassure them, while the conqueror was still plunging farther into the remote East, and the military forces of his enemy, supported by their powerful navy, were still accumulating in his rear. Nevertheless, his adherents removed the images of Pompeius and Sulla from the forum, and his secret enemies were controlled by spies, and required to join every demonstration of the general satisfaction. Then came the news of the death of Pompeius, attested by the exhibition of his ring to the citizens. Friends and enemies now combined to flatter the irresistible conqueror. Decrees were issued investing him with unlimited power to raise men and means for the suppression of the republicans, who were again making head in Africa. In October, B.C. 48, Cæsar was created, in his absence, dictator by the senate for the second time, while, for the satisfaction of the people, the powers of the tribunate were decreed to him for life. He appointed M. Antonius his master of the horse and commandant in the city. Brave, but violent and dissolute, Antonius lacked both sustained vigor and prudence. Sinister rumors began to circulate. Cæsar was in peril at Alexandria. Sedition raised her head, and Antonius shrank from the risk of failure in attacking it. Disturbances were excited by Cornelius Dolabella, a weak profligate, burdened with debts, a son-in-law of Cicero, who, like Cælius, raised the terrible cry of "New Tables," or an extinction of debts. Antonius summoned courage to repress the tumult, but not till Dolabella had personally affronted him. The demagogue had got himself adopted into a plebeian house in order to obtain the tribuneship, and he was allowed to enjoy the legal inviolability with which that office in vested him. In September, B.C. 47, Cæsar returned to Rome, and at once all men and all factions quailed before him.

Cæsar at Rome and third time dictator. U.C. 708. B.C. 46.—Mutiny of the Tenth legion suppressed.

The traditions of the civil wars pointed to a barbarous proscription; but the clemency of Cæsar was a star of hope to the citizens, and they were not disappointed in it. He was satisfied, at least, with seizing on the estates of the men who were still in arms against him, and with putting up to public sale the property of his great rival. The dictator remained only three months in Rome. He appointed consuls for the closing period of the year, and designated himself with Æmilius Lepidus for the year next ensuing. He caused himself to be again created dictator; the financial crisis had not yet passed, and, doubtless, a firm hand was required with competent powers to carry the commonwealth through it. He loaded his partisans with offices and honors, and sated the populace with largesses. This lavish expenditure of money seems to have been his chief means of government. But when his soldiers demanded the fulfilment of his golden promises, and his own favorite Tenth Legion broke out into mutiny, he sternly refused concession. Calling the soldiers together in the Campus Martius, he confronted them unattended, mounted his tribunal, and demanded the statement of their grievances. At the sight of their redoubted general their hearts failed, their voices faltered; they could only plead piteously for their discharge. "I discharge you, *citizens*!" replied the imperator. The effect of this last simple word was magical. To the fierce and haughty soldier the peaceful title of citizen seemed a degradation. He entreated to be restored to his standards, and offered to submit to military punishment. This striking anecdote is often cited to show the military pride of the great nation of warriors; but it testifies more particularly to the effect of the long period of warfare to which the soldier had been now so commonly subjected, and to the scorn which the professional swordsman too often feels elsewhere than in Rome for the name and character of civilian. The veterans of Camillus, of Scipio, perhaps even of Marius, would not have disdained to be addressed as Roman citizens.

The republicans transfer their forces to Africa.

Thus reassured of the force and temper of the weapon he wielded, Cæsar hastened away again to crush the gathering of his enemies assembled in the province of Africa. The defeated host had been scattered at Pharsalia in many directions; but the largest division of the fugitives had made its way to Dyrrhachium, and had there taken breath to concert its further movements. Cato, to whom the command was offered, waived it in favor of Cicero, the consular and the proconsul; but the orator declined to engage further in a struggle which he regarded as hopeless, and withdrew sorrowfully into Italy. Cnæus, the violent son of Pompeius, would have laid hands upon him, and he was glad to throw himself at last on Cæsar's clemency. Thereupon Scipio assumed the command, and carried the main body to Utica. Cato, at the head of another division, skirted the coasts of Greece and Asia, picking up some fleeing adherents of the cause. He followed in the track of Pompeius; but when informed of his chief's assassination he landed on the shore of Libya, and demanded admission into Cyrene. The natives shut their gates; but Cato respected their fears, and refrained from chastising them. Anxious now to effect a junction with Scipio, he coasted westward as far as the Lesser Syrtis, and then plunged with his little army into the sandy desert. The march through this torrid and trackless region occupied seven days, and was celebrated as an act of chivalrous endurance, which might raise the character of Cato above that of many victorious and triumphant imperators. The object of undertaking it is hard to comprehend; but in this as in many other details of Roman military history we must allow for our imperfect knowledge of the means available for the operations in hand. On joining the bulk of the republican forces in the Roman province, Cato was indignant at the position of his colleagues in command Scipio had sought the aid of Juba, king of Numidia, an ally and hitherto a dependent of the republic. But this prince had seized the opportunity to exalt his own importance, and presumed on the large resources he could bring, as well as on his recent services to the cause in his defeat of Curio, to take the first place in the republican councils. Cato was glad to escape from this humiliation by accepting a local command at Utica, the chief place in the province and the principal port for communication with Italy. Nor were his friends less willing to be relieved from his importunate susceptibilities. For a time, perhaps, they felt themselves secure from Cæsar's pursuit, for Cæsar was still deficient in naval resources. They forgot the loss of their great army and their still greater chief, and flattered themselves that victory was still in their hands. Labienus, the renegade, had now become their chief military adviser, while Scipio was surrounded by Afranius, Petreius, the sons of Pompeius, and other leaders of the party, all abundantly confident in themselves, and loud in denunciation of their enemy. But their military capacity was slender; of political vision they had none at all.

Cæsar's victory at Thapsus.
U.C. 708. B.C. 46.

Such was the posture of affairs in the republican camp, when Cæsar suddenly appeared off the coast with the small division of his troops for which he could secure means of transport, having evaded the vigilance of Scipio's fleet. He summoned the leaders of the force at Adrumetum to surrender to Cæsar "the imperator." They replied, "There is no imperator here but Scipio," and put his herald to death as a deserter. The dictator sailed on to Leptis, and landing there, with the good-will of the inhabitants, awaited further succors. There he was menaced by Scipio; and Labienus, who frequently led the 0pposing cavalry, flung bitter taunts at the veterans whom he had so often led to victory. But Cæsar maintained himself quietly within his entrenchments till he could move forward with five legions, while by making an alliance with the Mauretanians he was enabled to drive away Juba to the defence of his own capital. Scipio had no spirit to combat him alone. The republican force drew off; Cæsar advanced, and was rapidly gaining the upper hand. After a time Juba rejoined his friends, and made them feel that they had become more than ever dependent upon him. He forbade Scipio to wear the imperator's purple cloak, which pertained, he said, to kings only. At last, on April 4, the armies met on the field of Thapsus. Some of Cæsar's troops were fresh levies, and he was not sure of their steadiness; but the impetuosity of the redoubted Tenth legion forced on the battle, and carried the imperator along with it. Cæsar invoked his wonted good fortune, and spurring his horse took the lead of his battalions. The combat was soon decided. The Numidian elephants turned upon the ranks which they were placed to cover. The native cavalry, dismayed at the loss of their accustomed support, hastened to abandon the field. Scipio's legions made little resistance. Separated from their fleeing officers, they begged for quarter; but a frightful massacre was made of them, which Cæsar was unable to control. Scipio, escaping to the coast, was taken and slain. Juba and Petreius fled together and sought refuge in Zama, but the Numidians refused shelter to their tyrant and his companion. Thus repulsed, the fugitives first ate and drank together; then, in the spirit of barbarian gladiators, challenged each other to mortal combat. Petreius was first to fall in the duel; Juba threw himself on his own sword.

Death of Cato at Utica.

Cato was now left to defend himself alone in Africa. His own course had been long decided; but he allowed his followers to choose for themselves between submission, or flight, or resistance to the utmost. The senators and knights, despairing, it is said, of pardon, would have held out; but the traders and men of peace, long settled in Utica, had little to fear from yielding, and insisted on a timely surrender. Cato closed all the gates except that which opened upon the port, and urged his associates to take to the sea. With his son and a few devoted friends who refused to leave him he sat down to supper on the eve of Cæsar's arrival. He discoursed with more than his usual fervor on the highest themes of philosophy, especially on the generous paradox of the Stoics, that the good man alone is free, and all the bad are slaves. Meanwhile the embarkation was proceeding. Cato sent repeatedly to inquire who had already put to sea, and what were the prospects of the voyage. Retiring to his chamber he took up the "Dialogue on the Soul," in which Plato has recorded his dying master's last longing for immortality. Looking up, he observed that his sword had been removed. He sent for his friends, rebuked them for their unworthy precaution, "as if," he said, "he might not at any time kill himself by dashing his head against the wall, or merely by holding his breath." Reassured, perhaps, for a moment by the calmness of his demeanor, they restored him his weapon, and, at his earnest desire, left him once more alone. At midnight he inquired again about the departure of his followers. The last vessel, it was replied, was just leaving the quay. He then threw himself on his couch; but when all was quiet he seized his sword and thrust it into his body. The blow was not immediately mortal, and he rolled groaning on the floor. His attendants rushed in; a surgeon sewed up the gash. But on coming to himself, he repulsed his disconsolate friends, and, tearing open the wound, expired with the same dogged resolution which through life had distinguished him.

Character of Cato of Utica.

There is something so Roman, and at the same time so peculiar, in the character of this hero of ancient history that a few words may well be bestowed on Character of a special notice of it. Cato of Utica, as he is commonly called, to distinguish him from his great-grandfather, Cato the Censor, inherited from his ancestor the rugged disposition of the Sabine high landers. He was naturally harsh in temper, quaint in humor, strict in the discharge of duties interpreted in a narrow sense, enduring much himself and exacting no less of others. The elder Cato had struggled through life resisting the influence of Grecian ideas, which he deemed wholly pernicious, though in his latest years he had deigned at last to make himself acquainted with the Greek language. His descendant, after the lapse of a century, had yielded altogether to the new lights which had pervaded his country, and had received at least the outward polish of the literature and philosophy of the schools. The time had in fact just arrived when the more sensitive and sanguine spirits at Rome were beginning to throw off the blind devotion of a ruder age to mere form and ceremonial, and look into their own hearts for the moral resources which had become necessary to them. Cato himself was a religious enthusiast, but he was, in Roman phrase, full of the god within his own breast, and retained no external object of belief. From the time of Plato at least the philosophers of Greece had taught men to look into their own hearts for the rule of spiritual life. It was but recently that this subjective idea of religion had been introduced into Rome, where it met with little intelligent acceptance. For the most part, those among the Romans who most readily rejected the creed of antiquity, cast themselves on the tenets of the Epicureans, which were, in fact, a mere negation of religion altogether. Those who, like Cato, embraced the system of the Stoics, were even more rigid and pedantic in their notions than their masters, and of these none was more eminent for the strictness of his rule, and his devotion to his principle, than the philosophic statesman who gave up his life for his faith at Utica. Cato died for his religion as much as any martyr of the heathen or the Christian world; for he held it as a religious duty to maintain the constitution of his country; but the error or the vice of his system was that he acknowledged no duty to any Being exterior to himself, to whom he owed his existence, and for whom he was bound to support it. According to the severe logic of his false philosophy, when the republic had perished, his own work, though left undone, was, as far as he was concerned, practically finished. There was now no further place for him in life; wherefore he bowed to his destiny and quitted it without a murmur. The melancholy result of this error was that the pupils of Cato's school elevated it into a principle, and Seneca and others both defended and followed it.

CHAPTER VIII.
(U.C. 709. B.C. 45.—U.C. 710. B.C. 44.)

Tyranny and Death of Cæsar.

Honors conferred upon Cæsar at Rome.

THE suicide of Cato forms a dignified close to the liberties of Rome. Both in life and death he was a representative man; and viewing the subject from our point of view, we can hardly wish that the bravest champion of the ancient polity should have allowed his career to be protracted under the conditions which would have been thenceforth imposed upon it. Nevertheless, it is only just to the conqueror to observe that Cato had nothing to fear for his life or personal freedom under the dictator and imperator. Cæsar lamented that he had lost the satisfaction of pardoning him his treason to the constituted public authority, while to his comrades in arms he exhibited the same clemency which had so long distinguished him. Nevertheless, unnecessary and useless as this celebrated act of self-sacrifice may appear, it has done more, perhaps, to exalt the free-state and degrade the empire in the imagination of later generations than could have been effected by a supine or sullen acquiescence in evil fortune. A superstition has at times prevailed that an injured man, in committing suicide, may fasten an avenging demon on the author of his calamities. Stained with the blood of Rome's best son, the victor of Thapsus returned to his country vitiated and debased. The honors which a subservient senate now heaped upon him have lowered him in the eyes of posterity, even more than they exalted him in those of his contemporaries. After uniting to the African province a part of Numidia, and placing the remaining portion in the hands of his own allies, the dictator repaired once more to Italy at the end of July, B.C. 46. He was received as the conqueror of a foreign enemy. Statues rose in his honor. One fronted the altar of Jupiter in the Capitol; another stood on a globe, and was inscribed in the Greek language, for the idea was still

Hellenic only, to "Cæsar, the demi-god." The seventh month of the year, the fifth of the most ancient calendars, exchanged its name, Quintilis, for that of Julius. The dictatorship was now conferred upon Cæsar for ten years, and was presently settled upon him for life. He received the censorship under a slightly different title, which gave him power to revise the list of knights and senators, to degrade whom he would, to thrust whom he would into the highest orders of citizens. He was to nominate many of the chief magistrates hitherto elected by the people, and to appoint the governors of divers provinces, which had been the prerogative of the senate. The title of imperator was prefixed to his name; and the laurel wreath, which was given to him, it is said, to disguise his baldness, became a more signal symbol of power than the regal diadem, which alone was withheld from him. Nor was he ashamed to arrogate to himself the name of father of his country, the most glorious appellation a free people can bestow, which had been conferred by decree upon Camillus, by acclamation upon Cicero.

The title of Imperator prefixed.

Of all these titles the most remarkable was the prefix of Imperator, which has thus descended through many generations even to our own times, and still bears a political significance, as popularly conveying the idea of a despotic ruler. But such was by no means strictly the meaning attached to it by the Romans of the period before us. The "imperium" from which it was derived was no doubt the rule of a master; but this rule might be delegated by law and controlled by appropriate checks. The consul was himself subject to the law; nevertheless, he possessed the imperium for certain purposes, under the restraint of election by the people, and of eventual responsibility to them. The commander of a legion had the imperium, or military control, of his soldiers and of the province in which they served, and he received the title of imperator; but his authority was limited in place, in time, and in object. His title, conferred legitimately by the senate, was ratified by the less regular acclamations of his soldiers when he gained them a victory. The imperator of an army in a province abroad bore the title after his own name, as with any other limited magistracy. Cæsar, as proconsul of Gaul, was "Cæsar imperator" in relation to the legions with which he conquered Gaul. But when he became consul and dictator in the city he was no longer the ruler of a province or the commander of a provincial army. Chief of the state at home, he was at the same time engaged in the defence of the whole empire against foreign or domestic foes in every quarter. He was rendered by the force of circumstances commander-in-chief of all the legions, and his province was the empire itself. Such, it would seem, was the idea conveyed to the minds of the citizens by prefixing the title to his name instead of appending it. The distinction was real; it was invented to meet an actual need; and it was legitimately conferred by the senate itself, a subservient, no doubt, but still a constitutional body. The title so conferred bore little significance in the city. Cicero does not seem to make any reference to it. Cæsar did not stamp it on his coins. It was directed towards foes and foreigners, not towards the citizens. Some generations later, the reigning emperors could still insist warmly on the constitutional distinction between the "imperator over the soldiers," and "prince or premier among the citizens." This distinction was indeed too soon lost. The authority of the Imperator came to be regarded as supreme over every class and order in the state. But it should not be forgotten that Suetonius and Dion Cassius, who boldly assert that Cæsar himself received the title in token of his despotic sovereignty, speak in the sense of their own later times, and are no proper exponents of its original and legitimate signification.

Cæsar celebrates four triumphs.

Pompeius had triumphed thrice. Cæsar now claimed an accumulation of four triumphs; the first for his conquest of the Gauls; the second for his defeat of Ptolemæus; the third for his victory over Pharnaces the last for the overthrow of Juba. He condescended to respect the maxim of his countrymen, that a civil war can earn no such popular distinctions, and refrained from celebrating the public catastrophe at Pharsalia. These four solemnities were kept with a few days' interval between each. The procession formed again and again in the Campus. Hence it defiled through the triumphal gate at the foot of the Capitoline. In crossing the Velabrum the imperator's car broke down, a mischance which so affected him that he never again mounted a vehicle without muttering a charm. The long march wound round the southern angle of the Palatine to the point where the arch of

Constantine now stands. There it mounted the gentle slope which leads under the arch of Titus, paved at this day with huge blocks of stone which may possibly have echoed to the tramp of Cæsar's legions. Inclining to the right at the summit of the Velia and facing the Comitia and the Rostra, it passed the spot where the Julian temple was afterwards erected; thence it skirted the right side of the Forum till it reached the point just beyond the arch of Severus, where the two roads branched off, the one to the Capitoline temple, the other to the Mamertine prison. Cæsar took the route of triumph to the left, while his captive, Vercingetorix, was led away to the right, and strangled in the subterranean dungeon. The Gaulish hero doubtless met his fate with his well-tried courage and dignity, while his conqueror was exhibiting a wretched spectacle of human infirmity, crawling up the steps of the Capitol on his knees, to avert the wrath of an avenging Nemesis.

Cæsar's liberality to soldiers and citizens.

The Gaulish captive was undoubtedly slain. It is said that other victims perished with him, but the sons of Juba seem to have been spared; one of them at least survived as a tranquil student in the days of Augustus. Arsinoe, the sister of Ptolemæus and Cleopatra, was pardoned, perhaps for the sake of the dictator's paramour; for Cleopatra herself followed her admirer to Rome, and was there entertained by him in high state. The magnates of the city, even Cicero himself, courted her favor. The soldiers who attended on their general's chariot—men of strange tongues and countenances, Gauls, Spaniards, and Africans—chanted ribald songs with the license of the old Roman legionaries, in mockery of the leader whom they adored; he smiled and paid them their expected gratuity of 20,000 sesterces (200*l.*) a-piece. The largess was extended in due proportion to the whole body of the unarmed citizens, each of whom was well content with a present of 400. The people of Rome were entertained at a banquet spread on 22,000 tables, which may have accommodated guests. This festival was followed by shows in the amphitheatre and circus. The multitude of beasts and gladiators who were almost indiscriminately sacrificed moved some pity even in the brutalized populace; but the more thoughtful of them were doubly shocked by the license which Cæsar allowed to Roman knights of combating in the arena. It was all the worse, perhaps, that these combats were, it seems, almost wholly voluntary; the violence of the times had engendered a thirst for violence and bloodshed. Laberius, a knight who was required thus to exhibit himself, complained of the indignity to himself, but took no thought of its inhumanity.

The Julian Forum.

Cæsar had long since commenced a great reconstruction of the interior of the city. The ancient Forum was contracted in space, and the population had far outgrown the accommodation it afforded. Cæsar had indeed himself erected his noble basilica on one side of it, and encouraged Æmilius Paulus to confine it with another, not less sumptuous, directly opposite. Such large halls were of great convenience to the crowds who met together for public business in an open area exposed to all the vicissitudes of climate. But the area itself required to be enlarged, and the dictator had cleared away some buildings on its northern side, enclosing the space thus acquired with colonnades, and opening an entrance into it. The Julian Forum, as this area was denominated was adorned with a temple of Venus "the ancestress," from whom the Julian family was reputed to have sprung, and with an equestrian statue of the imperator himself—really a bronze effigy of Alexander the Great, by Lysippus, with a new head to it—which became one of the most notable features of the great city. Succeeding emperors—Augustus, Nerva, and Trajan—made fresh additions to these public areas, each giving his own name to the Forum of his own construction, till the centre of Rome was expanded into one large open space, divided only by public halls and temples.

War in Spain and battle of Munda, U.C. 709. B.C. 45.

While the issue of the African campaign was yet undecided, Cnæus, the elder son of Pompeius, had thrown himself into the Iberian peninsula, in which his father's interest was still strong, and had there proclaimed himself, not the liberator the commonwealth, but the avenger of his family's wrongs. He had gathered around him adventurers of various kinds. Many even of

Cæsar's veterans, dissatisfied with their rewards, had betaken themselves to his standard, and some of the southern cities of the province had lent him the shelter of their walls Cæsar refused to recognize this new assailant as a legitimate enemy; but when his officers failed to suppress the spirit of brigandage which animated the rebel host, he at last took the field in person, and allowed himself to treat them, not as citizens, but as outlaws or barbarians. Cnæus, indeed, had set the example of ferocity, for of all the leaders of the civil wars this man seems to have been the most sanguinary and brutal. The contest was carried on mainly in the valley of the Guadalquivir and the defiles of the Sierra Morena. The struggle, protracted for several months, was closed, however, on the field of Munda, where Cæsar, after encountering great personal danger, gained at last a complete victory. Thirty thousand of the vanquished party perished among them were Varus and Labienus, with many other nobles. Cnæus escaped from the field, gained the coast, and put out to sea; but being forced to land to get relief for an accidental hurt, having cut his foot in releasing himself from a tangled rope, he was discovered and killed, after a miserable struggle. Of all the republican leaders, Sextus, the younger son of Pompeius, was now the sole survivor in arms. He hid himself in the wildest districts of the peninsula, making alliance with roving bands of natives, till occasion served for reappearing, after some interval, on the public scene. For a time, however, he was forgotten or neglected. Cæsar devoted some months to arranging the affairs of the western provinces, and thoroughly crushing the republican faction in that quarter. The battle of Munda had been fought on March 17, but the conqueror was not at liberty to return to Italy before September.

The Roman Calendar requires correction.

In the following month Cæsar celebrated a fifth triumph, which he pretended to have gained, not over the citizens and the chiefs of the party opposed to him, but over the still unconquered natives of the Iberian peninsula. He then proceeded to address himself to domestic reforms and projects of public benefit, of which a general outline will be here sufficient. Among the first was the revision of the Calendar, a matter of great concern, political as well as scientific. The Calendar of Numa, as it was called, hitherto in use, had assigned to the year a period of 354 days, with the intercalation every second year of a month of 22 and 23 days alternately, which would have given an average of 365 days and 6 hours: so near had the ancient astronomers arrived to the precise length of the earth's revolution round the sun. But another day, it seems, had been added to the 354, to make an odd or fortunate number; and to compensate for this excessive addition, the number of intercalations was diminished by an intricate process. Much carelessness had prevailed in making the requisite corrections. The pontiffs to whom the duty had been entrusted had abused it for political objects, to favor the candidature of a partisan, or to postpone the day when his debts might be demanded. The control of the Calendar had become an engine of state in the hands of the oligarchy, and constituted one of the grievances of the plebs. But latterly, in the general confusion of affairs, the pontiffs had generally abstained from intercalation. The year had been restricted to its 354 days; the designated months and seasons had fallen far into arrear of the solar time. So it was that the consuls who were appointed to enter upon office on the 1st of January, B.C. 46 (U.C. 708), actually commenced their functions on the 13th of October, B.C. 47. The Roman seasons were marked by appropriate festivals on certain fixed days. At the period of harvest and vintage, seasonable offerings were to be made accordingly; and this had now become no longer possible. The husbandman was reduced to reject the use of the Calendar altogether, and to depend on his own rude observations of the rising and setting of the constellations.

The reformed or Julian Calendar.

But Cæsar had acquired a competent knowledge of astronomical science, and discerned at the same time how popular a use he could make of it. He availed himself, moreover, of the services of Sosigenes, the ablest astronomer of the day, who divided the 365 days of the old Calendar among the twelve months in the order they have since retained, and intercalated a single day, as we still do, every fourth year. Some error in the working of this system, which was not attributable to himself, caused another slight correction to be made a few years later. It was not for several centuries that the further error was discovered, and finally reformed, by dropping this intercalation on the recurrence of certain centennial years, as decreed by Pope Gregory XIII., and accepted in this country in the middle of the last century. As regarded the actual crisis at which the Roman Calendar had arrived, Cæsar added as many as 90 days to the year of the city, 709, or B.C. 45. He inserted an intercalary month of 23 days between the 23rd and 24th of February; and at the end of November he added two new months, each of 30 days, together with a supplemental addition of 7 days more. The whole period thus comprised 355+90, or 445 days. Marked by this series of alterations, it received vulgarly the appellation of the "year of confusion" but the "last year of confusion," it has been justly remarked, would be its more appropriate title.

Measures for extending the franchise, increasing the senate, &c.—Appointment to offices.

During the whole of this long year the dictator continued to preside over affairs at the centre of the empire, and with his new enactments and projects rendered it perhaps the most illustrious in the Roman annals. His measures were principally directed to the enfranchisement of communities, of classes, and of individuals, by which continued process he meditated the gradual fusion of the provinces into the city itself. He added largely to the numbers of the senate, which had been no doubt much reduced by the massacres of the civil wars. We hear, indeed, of the senate dividing once or twice just before this period, to the number of more than 400; but Cæsar increased it at once to 900. Doubtless he lowered the popular estimation of the august assembly by thus cheapening its honors; but he still more degraded it in the eyes of the older citizens by pouring into it his allies from the provinces, his rude Gaulish soldiers, and even, if we may believe the stories of the day, the captives who had just followed his triumph. The Romans exercised their wit on these upstart strangers losing themselves among the columns of the Forum, and posted placards recommending that no good citizen should show them the way to the senate-house. But the policy of abating the pride of the oligarchy, and attaching foreigners to the state by opening to them its honors, deserved a deliberate and a patient trial, which, in fact, it never received. The same populace who mocked or resented this intrusion were willing to surrender to the great conqueror their own privilege of appointment to all public offices;

and he could hardly prevail upon them to give, by their votes in the Campus, even a color of free election to the men whom he recommended. The consuls, prætors, and other officers continued to exercise their ordinary functions under the dictator's superintendence. But as the avowed champion of the people, Cæsar claimed the distinction of the tribunician power, which also rendered his person legally inviolable, and invested it with a certain religious sanctity in the eyes of the multitude. He allowed himself to be surrounded by a body-guard of noble citizens, elsewhere the august privilege of kings only. In the senate and other public places he seated himself on a golden chair, in a robe of regal magnificence, and the imperium, or military supremacy which had been given him for his own life, was rendered, if we may believe some later writers, transmissible to his children. Issue, indeed, of his own he had none, unless Cæsario, the child of Cleopatra, was really his; and perhaps even the servile populace would have shrunk from giving themselves a master in the baseborn offspring of a foreigner and an Egyptian. But Cæsar had a nephew, the promising young son of his sister by a Roman noble, who will soon come prominently upon the stage.

Cæsar founds colonies.—Further projects. Survey of the empire.—Codification of the law.

But we return to the projects of the great dictator during the course of the year which, under happier auspices, might have really become the last of civil strife and political confusion. The military statesmen of Rome had generally adopted one of two plans for relieving the impoverished classes of the city, and drafting off from Rome itself the superfluous masses of its soldiery. Pompeius and Sulla had seized upon the forfeited estates of their adversaries throughout the peninsula, and planted their veterans upon them; but the effect of these forcible assignments had been generally disastrous. They had embittered strife and engendered perpetual animosities among the sufferers, while they had demoralized the men whom they were meant to serve, and rendered them both idle and turbulent. Cæsar reverted to the ancient method of settling new colonies of Roman citizens, and he selected, from policy or generosity, some of the cities which had suffered most from their rivalry with Rome, and of which Rome had up to this time never ceased to be jealous. He proposed thus to restore Corinth, Capua, and Carthage; and all his colonies, thus wisely chosen, grew and flourished, and became in after ages some of the noblest cities of the empire. Corinth significantly adopted the name of *Laus Julia*; perhaps she looked forward from the first to the project he already contemplated, of cutting through the isthmus, and thus mingling in one harbor the commerce of eastern and western Greece, of Europe and of Asia. The liberal views which the dictator entertained for the extension of the Roman franchise might lead him to regard Rome herself as no longer an isolated municipium, but the centre and capital of the Roman world. As be proceeded to lay the groundwork of a comprehensive scheme of universal legislation, his first care was to develop the material unity of the vast regions before him by an elaborate survey of their local relations. The Roman land-measurers were accustomed to draw the boundaries of public and private estates. Italy and the provinces were to a great extent marked out by their terminal stones and limits. A commission of geographers and mathematicians was now appointed to execute a survey of the whole empire, a work of labor which seems to have been steadily continued, even through the turbulent years that followed, till it issued in the great map of Agrippa a whole generation later. Another effort, not less gigantic, was required to impress a moral unity upon this mighty machine. Cæsar prepared to collect and combine in a single code the fragments of Roman law, dispersed in a multitude of precedents, in the edicts of prætors, the replies of counsellors, the decisions of pontiffs, and the traditions of patrician houses. No doubt he would have completed this undertaking by bringing the laws and customs of the various provinces into working harmony with those of the ruling city, and adjusting the ever-conflicting pretensions of the Roman and the subject before the tribunals at home and abroad. Such an important work had been already imagined by Cicero as the hope less vision of the philanthropic philosopher; but Cæsar's practical sagacity saw that it not only ought to be done, but could be done; and it is possible that, had he lived ten or twenty years longer, he would have anticipated by six centuries the peaceful glory of Justinian.

Cæsar projects the extensions of the walls, etc.

To these may be added some great material works which the dictator projected nearer home. He was ambitions of advancing the pomœrium, or sacred limit within which the auspices could be taken; and he would probably have given a greater circuit to the walls of Rome, which had never been extended since the early demarkation of Servius, and were now thrown down or obliterated in many quarters. He would have reconstructed a real line of defence embracing the Campus Martius; and the Campus itself he would have enlarged by turning the Tiber westward with a bold sweep from the Milvian to the Vatican bridge. Further, he planned, it is said, the emptying of the lake Fucinus, the draining of the Pomptine marshes, the construction of a canal from Rome to Tarracina, a new road across the Apennines, and a capacious harbor at Ostia; a grand combination of schemes to be conceived at one moment by one head, the utility of which was perceived by his successors, and most of which were actually accomplished by them in the course of after ages.

Abortive attempts to give Cæsar the title of king.

The heir whom Cæsar destined for the imperium was already in the camp at Apollonia. This young man was C. Octavius, the son of Atia, daughter of the dictator's sister, Julia, who was now (at the beginning of B.C. 44) in his nineteenth year. Cæsar had promoted his house from the plebeian to the patrician order. He allowed it further to be understood that he meant to make him his own son by adoption, and bequeath to him his patrimony, together with the dignities which the senate had declared hereditary in his family. These dignities, indeed, were not hitherto associated in the minds of the Romans with any ideas of hereditary succession. They could hardly conceive the descent of the dictatorship, for instance, from the hands of mature experience to those of an untried youth, or the establishment of the tribunician power, the free gift of the people, in the line of a particular family. They would naturally conclude that their hero was intent on securing a title, on which alone, in their view, a dynasty could be founded. Cæsar, it was reported, desired to be hailed as *king*. His flatterers suggested it, his enemies readily believed it, and hoped to make him unpopular by urging him to advance the claim. One morning a laurel garland, with a diadem attached, was found affixed to his statue before the Rostra. The tribunes indignantly tore it down, the populace expressing satisfaction at their conduct, and saluting them with acclamations as the modern Brutuses. Cæsar affected at least to applaud them.

When a second attempt of the same kind was made, and the people again murmured, he hastily exclaimed, "I am no king, but Cæsar." He began now, however, to show some signs of mortification; but his friends, if such were the real promoters of the intrigue, still thought the prize within his reach. On the 18th of February, the day of the Lupercalia, the imperator was presiding in his golden chair before the Rostra. His devoted follower, M. Antonius, took a prominent part in the solemnity, running, lightly clad, through the streets, with a thong in his hand, with which he struck the women who presented themselves to receive the blow, which was reputed to avert barrenness. When he had run his course he broke through the excited throng, and, drawing from his girdle a diadem, made as if he would offer it to Cæsar, exclaiming that it was the gift of the Roman people. Some clapping of hands ensued, but it was faint and brief, and manifestly preconcerted. When Cæsar put away from him the proffered gift, the applause was hearty and spontaneous. "I am not king," he repeated; "the only king of the Romans is Jupiter." He ordered the diadem to be carried to the Capitol and suspended in the temple, to commemorate the gracious offer of the people and his own patriotic refusal.

Conspiracy against Cæsar.

This discretion baffled the visions that might be entertained of a popular rising against the usurper; but feelings of distrust and despair were taking possession of many of the more eminent citizens, and were not confined to the remnant of the republican party. Some, no doubt, were disappointed in their hopes of preferment under the new administration; but others, who had been advanced to high office, still felt aggrieved at the pre-eminence which had been attained by one whom they refused to regard as more than an equal; and no doubt the prospect of such pre-eminence being transmitted to an inconsiderable stripling added a fresh sting to their vexation. A plot against Cæsar's life was now deliberately formed. The secret was shared among sixty or even eighty conspirators, some of them the most familiar and the most trusted of his personal friends. Decimus Brutus, Trebonius, Casca, and Cimber, had all received distinguished marks of the dictator's favor. C. Cassius professed himself a republican; yet, he too, had avowed his preference for the merciful Cæsar over the fierce and sanguinary sons of Pompeius. But he was a man of bitter and jealous temper; a restless intriguer, without a scruple or a principle. He worked upon the simpler and kindlier nature of M. Junius Brutus, a weak follower of his uncle the sturdy Cato, whom he professed to make his example in philosophy and also in civic virtue. Brutus was willing, however, to accept the important government of the Cisalpine from the hands of the dictator, and acquiesced without a murmur in the political situation. The weakness of his character may be estimated from the means which the conspirators employed to influence him. They affixed a paper to the statue of the elder Brutus, with the words, "Would thou wert alive." They thrust billets into his hand inscribed, "Brutus, thou sleepest; thou art no longer Brutus." But they rightly calculated the effect of his name in their ranks, which seemed to give a distinct aim to the undertaking, and to invest it with a patriotic color.

Cæsar assassinated, March 15, U.C. 710. B.C. 44.

The intrigue soon ripened to its execution. Cæsar had assumed the consulship, together with M. Antonius, and had announced, at the commencement of the year, his intention of leading a great force into the East to avenge the slaughter of Crassus, and of triumphing over the rival kingdom of Parthia. He even meditated, it is said, to return by the northern coast of the Euxine and crush the hostile league with which Mithridates had threatened to knit together the barbarians beyond the Danube. The preparations for the imperator's departure was almost complete. The senate was convened for the Ides of March, the 15th of the month. On this day, as soon as he should enter the Curia, the blow was to be struck. The 17th of that month was the day on which Pompeius had quitted the shores of Italy; the 17th was also the day of Cæsar's crowning victory at Munda; but the popular imagination seems to have antedated an anniversary of so much note in the hero's career, and the prediction was already current that the Ides of March should be fatal to him. Hitherto he had spurned every warning of danger; the easiest death, he had been recently heard to say, is that which comes most unexpectedly. He had even dismissed the guard which the senate had assigned for the protection of his person. So far he had refused to take any precautions. But his consort Calpurnia had a bad dream; the victims presented evil omens. At the last moment he seemed to hesitate. On the other side, Marcus Brutus was not less moved, and was sustained in his resolution only by the constancy of his wife, the noble Porcia, the daughter of Cato. Decimus Brutus, with more nerve, still urged Cæsar to present himself in the senate-house, and made a jest of his scruples. Cæsar advanced; but as he proceeded along the Forum towards the theatre of Pompeius in the Campus, more than one person pressed, it is said, upon him, to warn him of his danger. One, indeed, thrust a paper into his hand, and implored him to read it instantly. But he paid no heed, and held it still rolled up unread when he arrived at the hall of assembly. "The Ides of March are come," he observed complacently to the augur Spurinna. "Aye," muttered the sage, "but they are not yet passed." He entered the hall, his enemies closing around him and keeping his friends aloof, Trebonius being specially charged to detain Antonius at the door. On taking his seat, Cimber approached with a petition for his brother's pardon. The others, as was concerted, joined in the supplication, seizing his hands and embracing his neck. Cæsar at first put them gently aside; they redoubled their urgency; Cimber grasped his toga with both hands, and pulled it over his arms. Then Casca, who was behind, drew his stylus, or a dagger concealed in its case, and grazed his shoulder with an ill-directed stroke. Cæsar disengaged one hand with a cry, and snatched at the hilt. "Help!" cried Cæsar, and at the moment the others drew, and aimed each his dagger at their victim. Cæsar for an instant defended himself, and even wounded one of his assailants with his stylus; but when he noticed Brutus in the press, and saw the steel flashing in his band also, "What! thou too, Brutus!" he exclaimed, let go his grasp of Casca, and drawing his robe over his face, made no further resistance. The assassins stabbed him with thirty wounds, and he fell dead at the foot of Pompeius' statue.

Remarks on the character of Julius Cæsar.

Cæsar was assassinated in his fifty-sixth year. He was hacked to death with three-and-twenty blows, of which one only, it was said, would have been in itself mortal. In early life his health was delicate, and he was subject to epileptic fits, which attacked him in his African campaign, and again before the battle of Munda. Yet the energy and rapidity of his movements seem to prove the general robustness of his constitution. Had he escaped the stroke of the assassin he might probably have attained old age, and carried out himself the liberal schemes which he left to be more or less mutilated by a successor in the empire a quarter of a century later.

The name of Julius Cæsar has filled a larger space in secular history than any other. Such has been the effect produced on the imagination of posterity both by the greatness of the work which he accomplished and by the intrinsic greatness of his own character. The reduction of the unwieldy commonwealth of Rome under a single autocrat was doubtless an abortive effort, terminating in the premature death of its author and the overthrow of his government. It is easy to say that it was not Cæsar but Augustus after him that established the Roman empire. Nevertheless, the man who first conceives and executes a great design may command more attention from mankind than one who works upon his lines, and brings his designs to completion; and so it is that from generation to generation men have been wont to regard the immortal Julius as the first of the Cæsars and the first of the Roman emperors. To him as their political parent the great autocrats of Europe have ever since affiliated themselves; to the imperial rule derived from him modern civilization, it must he confessed, has been largely indebted, till it has ripened in a few favored communities into constitutional monarchies, and returned only here and there to the republican type out of which it emerged. The part which Cæsar has played in the development of human society through so many centuries must make him still the most conspicuous of all the actors on the world's stage before us.

Our estimate of this great man's actual ability stands on another footing, and must be referred simply to the definite judgment pronounced upon it by the historians. While other illustrious men have been reputed great for their excellence in some one department of intellect, the concurrent voice of antiquity has declared that Cæsar was excellent in all. "He had genius," says Cicero, "understanding, memory, taste, reflection, industry, and exactness." "He was great," repeats Drumann, "in everything he undertook; as a captain, a statesman, a lawgiver, a jurist, an orator, a poet, an historian, a grammarian, a mathematician, an architect." Pliny tells us that he could devote his mind without distraction to several subjects at once; he could write, dictate, and listen at the same moment. At the same time we are assured that in all the exercises of the camp his vigor and address were not less conspicuous. He fought at the most perilous moments in the ranks of the soldiers; he could manage his charger without the use of reins; he saved his life at Alexandria by his skill in the art of swimming. But of all his talents his personal influence over men seems to have been the most effective. Of all great men he seems to have been personally the most amiable, and to have retained the respect and love of his fellows notwithstanding a laxity of principle which shocked even his own corrupt times. And this is, perhaps, the more singular, inasmuch as Cæsar is pourtrayed to us as singularly devoid of the impulsiveness and enthusiasm which so often extort our forgiveness for grave moral delinquencies. But it is evident that none came in contact with him without succumbing to the charm of his superior intelligence, of his courage, his sense, his unerring judgment, still more, perhaps, of his unfailing success. The deep-rooted selfishness of his personal ambition was lost, it may be presumed, on a generation of unblushing self-seekers.

But it is as a general that Cæsar stands, after all, most pre-eminent; the common voice of antiquity has been echoed by many of the greatest commanders of modern times, and we may regard his military fame as legitimately established. Neither he himself, in his own commentaries, nor his lieutenant, who continued them, makes the slightest effort to disguise his occasional failures, or the straits to which they reduced him. All commanders have made such mistakes; but it is the special praise of Cæsar that his mistakes always tended to bring out the extent and variety of his resources, and to show the depth and deliberate character of his plans. The blows inflicted on him by the Treviri and by Vercingetorix prepared the way for his final conquest of Gaul; the repulse at Petra brought the civil war to a crowning triumph at Pharsalia; the check at Alexandria resulted in the subjugation of the richest kingdom of the East. It was not so with Hannibal; it was not so with Napoleon.

CHAPTER IX.
(U.C.710. B.C. 44.)

CAIUS OCTAVIUS SUCCEEDS TO THE INHERITANCE OF JULIUS CÆSAR.

Antonius makes his escape.

WHEN the conspirators looked round the hall was already empty. The senators had fled with precipitation. Centurions, lictors, and attendants had vanished with them, and the harangue which Brutus proposed to deliver found no hearers. Antonius had slipped through the crowd, exchanged clothes with a slave, and made his way to his own house on the Carinæ. Among the citizens there was general consternation, none knowing on whom the next blow might fall, or which party would be the first to resort to riot and massacre. Both had arms within reach. On the one hand Decimus Brutus had provided for the defence of his friends by placing some gladiators hard by in the Pompeian theatre; on the other, the city was filled with the dictator's veterans, and Lepidus, his master of the horse, commanded a legion outside the walls.

Antonius seizes on Cæsar's papers and effects.

The assassins now marched forth, brandishing their bloody weapons, and wrapping their gowns about their left arms as a defence against a sudden attack. They reached the Forum, preceded by a cap of liberty hoisted on a spear, exclaiming that they had slain a king and a tyrant. The place was filled with an agitated crowd, but these cries met with no response among them. Disconcerted by this indifference, the liberators, as they now called themselves, retired hastily to secure a place of refuge on the Capitoline. Here, with the aid of the gladiators of Decimus, they barred the gates of the enclosure. In the evening some of the nobles came to join them; among these was Cicero, who, though previously unconnected with the conspiracy, recovered hope from its first success, and advised that the senate should be convened immediately. But Brutus preferred to make another appeal to the feelings of the populace. On the morrow he descended into the Forum. To him indeed, personally, the people listened with respect; but against others who next addressed them they broke out into violence, and drove the whole party back to their place of shelter. Meanwhile Antonius had not been idle; he had communicated secretly with Calpurnia, and obtained possession of her husband's private treasure, and also of his will. With the aid of his two brothers, one a prætor, the other a tribune, he opened, as consul, the national coffers in the temple of Ops, and drew thence a store of coin with which he made advances to Lepidus, and received promises of support.

Antonius as consul convenes the senate.—
An amnesty decreed, March 17.

M. Antonius, who is now coming prominently to the front, had been hitherto slightly regarded as minister and companion of Cæsar; but from this moment he assumed in many eyes the position of his natural successor. Hitherto known chiefly for his amours and his dissipation, he was now about to display the arts of a consummate politician. Cicero stood alone in dissuading the liberators from negotiating with him. But they believed in his professions of loyalty, and hoped to gain an ascendency over the pliant temper which had always yielded to the influence of the dictator. It was agreed that as consul he should convene the senate for the next day, the 17th of March. He appointed for the place of meeting the temple of Tellus, near the Forum, which be filled with armed soldiers. The liberators dared not leave the Capitol, and the discussion of their fatal deed was carried on in their absence. The majority of the fathers would have stigmatized Cæsar as a tyrant, and thereby justified his assassination; but when Antonius represented that this would be to annul his acts and appointments, Dolabella and others interested in them resisted the decree with all their might. While the senators still deliberated, Antonius went forth into the Forum. The people hailed him with acclamations, bidding him at the same time beware for his own life. The senators were uneasy at this demonstration, and Cicero pointed out to them the only course that could relieve them with dignity from their embarrassment. He demanded an *amnesty*, or act of oblivion, which should simply confirm every existing appointment, and leave the deed of the conspirators to the judgment of posterity. In private he had declared himself a warm approver of the tyrannicide; but he now confessed in his public acts that the peace of the city and the interests of the senate required a compromise. An amnesty was decreed. The next day Cicero harangued and calmed the populace. The liberators were invited to descend from their place of refuge, Lepidus and Antonius sending them their own children as hostages, and the one entertaining Brutus, the other Cassius at supper. Antonius and Cassius were rude men, and some rude repartees passed between them. "Have you still a dagger under your arm?" asked the one. "Yes, truly," replied the other; "to slay you with if you aspire to the tyranny." Next morning all parties met again in the Curia, and the dictator's assignment of provinces was confirmed. Trebonius succeeded to Asia, Cimber to Bithynia, Decimus to the Cisalpine, while Macedonia was secured to Marcus Brutus, and Syria to Cassius, on the expiration of their office as prætors at home.

Antonius master of the situation.—Cæsar's funeral.—Popular excitement against the liberators.

Notwithstanding the power thus surrendered to the republican leaders, Antonius was still master of the situation. Since Cæsar was not "a tyrant," and his "acts" were sustained as legitimate, his testament must be accepted, and his remains honored with a public funeral. Antonius recited to the people their favorite's last will. He had adopted for his son the youthful Octavius; he had endowed the Roman people with his gardens on the bank of the Tiber, and bequeathed to every citizen 300 sesterces. This liberality warmed the feelings of the excitable multitude in his favor. The funeral pyre had been constructed in the Campus, but the eulogy of the deceased was to be pronounced in the Forum. A shrine, glittering with gold, was erected before the Rostra, in which the body was laid upon a couch of gold and ivory; at its head was suspended, like a warrior's trophy, the toga in which the hero had been slain, hacked by the assassins' daggers. The actual remains were indeed concealed from public gaze; but they were replaced by a waxen figure, on which his three-and-twenty wounds were faithfully represented. Dramatic shows formed, as usual, a part of the funeral ceremony, and the sensibilities of the people were moved by the scenic effect of the deaths of Agamemnon and Ajax, caused by the treason or cruelty of their nearest and dearest. When they were thus melting with compassion or glowing with resentment, Antonius stepped forward, as the chief magistrate of the republic, to recite the praises of the mighty dead. He read the decrees which had been heaped on Cæsar, declaring his person inviolate, his authority supreme, himself the chief and father of his country; and then he pointed to the bleeding corpse, which neither laws nor oaths had shielded from outrage. Lastly, with a movement toward the Capitol, he shouted: "I at least am prepared to keep my vow, to avenge the victim I could not save!" The people had been gradually worked up to feelings of fanatic devotion. They forbade the body to be carried outside the city; they insisted that it should be burnt within the walls. Chairs, tables, and benches, were snatched from the adjacent buildings, a heap of fuel was raised before the pontiff's dwelling in the Forum, and the body hastily placed upon it. The temple of Castor and Pollux stood hard by, on the spot where the two majestic warriors in olden time had announced the victory of Regillus. Now also two youths, of august mien and countenance, girt with swords and javelin in hand, were seen to apply the torch. A divine sanction was thus given to the deed; every scruple was overruled. The people continued to pile up brushwood, the veterans added their arms, the matrons their ornaments; even the trinkets on the children's frocks were cast into the fire. Cæsar was beloved by the Romans; he was not less dear to the foreigners. Gauls, Iberians, Africans and Orientals crowded around the pile, and gave vent to their sense of the common calamity. The success of Antonius was complete. The populace soon lashed themselves into fury, rushed through the streets with blazing brands, and tried to fire the houses of the conspirators. Their rude assaults were for the moment repulsed; but Brutus and his associates dared not show themselves in public, and either escaped from the city or lay concealed within it.

M. Antonius takes command in the city.

It was plain that the cause of the liberators was lost at the centre of the commonwealth. The populace raged against them while the chief of their party in the senate shrank from assisting them or vindicating their deed. Antonius acted with consummate craft in the use he made of the amnesty which the senators had decreed. He proposed that Sextus, the last surviving son of the great Pompeius, should be invited to return to Rome and assume such a place at the head of his father's friends as they should now choose to grant him. He was well aware, perhaps, that Sextus, in command of his maritime forces, had other ends in view, and that the name of Pompeius had lost all influence over the republican party in the senate. But the proposal seemed at least conciliatory, and might be taken as a token of political moderation. A still more politic stroke was the resolution which he carried for abolishing for ever the office and title of dictator, a magistracy not less odious to the senate now than it had formerly been to the people. But among the excited multitude of the Forum an era of turbulence and sedition had set in. The assassination of their favorite, Cæsar, was the pretext rather than the actual cause of the tumults with which they continued to agitate the city. Antonius made these disturbances an excuse for surrounding himself with a body-guard under the sanction of the senate itself, and this force he soon raised to an army of 6,000 men, with which he effectually kept peace in the streets. A low impostor, named Amatius, pretending to be a kinsman of Marius and Cæsar, had tried to ingratiate himself with the populace. The consuls opposed him with energy, overthrew him, and put him to death. Their zeal in defence of the republic was blindly applauded by the senate. Even Cicero, though he still utterly distrusted Antonius, could exclaim that his colleague Dolabella was the best and bravest of magistrates.

"The tyranny still survives."

The senate had confirmed Cæsar's acts. Antonius contrived that this confirmation should be extended to the public measures which the dictator had contemplated even though they had not yet been carried into effect. Armed with this sweeping decree, he proceeded to forge authority for every project he had himself in view. Laws, treasures, magistracies, all now lay at his feet. Things which the dictator had not dared himself to do Antonius carried into execution in his name. He sold preferments and provinces, retrieved his own dilapidated fortunes, and purchased the support of senators, soldiers, and tributary sovereigns. Under pretence of carrying out Cæsar's latest intentions, he reversed the appointments which Cæsar had actually made, and broke his recent engagement to the liberators in depriving Brutus and Cassius of their promised governments. Syria he assigned to Dolabella in reward for his opportune support; Macedonia, with the legions which Cæsar had mustered at Apollonia, be seized for himself. The rule of one man was absolute throughout the empire. "The tyrant is dead," sorrowfully murmured Cicero, "but the tyranny still lives." The tyranny still survived in the person of the consul; but the consul, it might be urged, had been popularly appointed, his term of office was fixed and brief; at the end of a year at furthest he must descend into the ranks of the private citizens. It still remained to be seen whether autocratic powers thus strictly limited could be indefinitely extended in the person of a man who possessed no claims to the support of nobles or commons, of provincials or allies. Never yet had any pretender to sovereignty at Rome essayed the crime with so little personal influence in his favor. But if Antonius should succeed to the province of Macedonia, and to the command of the legions of the great Cæsar, he would have the material instrument of power in his hand, and all political calculations must depend upon the disposition of this omnipotent soldiery.

C. Octavius arrives in Italy.
U.C. 710. B.C. 44.

Antonius was a bold and sanguine man, resolute in act and confident in his powers; but in forecasting the issue of his daring intrigue he proved after all mistaken. C. Octavius had spent some months among the legions at Apollonia, and the address with which he had attached them to himself gave token of the genius he was about to display on a wider theatre. Surprised amidst his juvenile exercises by the news of his uncle's assassination, he was not yet aware of the perilous inheritance which had been settled upon him. But his mother's letters from Rome, reminding him of the dictator's favor and of his nearness to him in blood, inflamed his hopes, and determined him to return at once to the city and brave every danger. His friends would have dissuaded him; but the soldiers nearest at hand, moved by the name of their hero Cæsar, pledged themselves to support him. Without a moment's hesitation the audacious stripling threw himself almost alone on the coast of Apulia. Here he received a copy of Cæsar's will, as well as of the senate's recent decrees. Thereupon he assumed his legitimate designation of Caius Julius Cæsar Octavianus, and presented himself to the garrison of Brundisium as the adopted son of the great imperator. By these soldiers he was saluted with enthusiasm; the friends and freed men of the dictator flocked around him; the veterans of the colonies drew their swords and offered to avenge his parent's assassination. But the young adventurer was cautious as well as bold. He declined the use or the display of force while he was yet uncertain of the course to be pursued. With rare self-command, he contented himself with addressing the senate in mild and temperate language, claiming as a private citizen the inheritance of a deceased father. Arriving at Cumæ, he learnt that Cicero was sojourning in the neighborhood. He went to visit the desponding patriot, and assured him of the loyal moderation of his own views. The veteran but too facile statesman was at once captivated, and persuaded himself that the son and heir of the great usurper was a faithful child of the republic. At the end of April, just six weeks from the dictator's death, the young Cæsar entered Rome. Antonius was absent at the moment, soliciting the adherence of fresh allies throughout the peninsula, and disgusting even the lax morality of his countrymen by the bold and coarse licentiousness of his private conduct. The royal progress which he made in company with the Grecian courtesan Cytheris was a fitting prelude to the splendor of his ignominious amours, which were to follow, with the Egyptian Cleopatra, and degraded him to the lowest pitch in the estimation of the patriots and moralists of Rome.

He assumes Cæsar's inheritance.

Octavius, as it may still be convenient to call the young aspirant to the name and fortunes of Cæsar, was at this time less than nineteen years of age; but neither his mother, Atia, nor his stepfather, Philippus, could dissuade him from claiming his inheritance. He presented himself before the prætor, and avowed himself the son and heir of the dictator. He mounted the tribune, and harangued the people, pledging himself to discharge the sums bequeathed them by his father, which Antonius had failed to do. But the consul felt no alarm. He cared not to return to Rome before the middle of May, and left the field of intrigue open to his diligent rival for one important month. Octavius turned every instant to account, making many friends and conciliating many enemies, till he felt himself strong enough to upbraid Antonius openly with his remissness in prosecuting the assassins. At the same time he publicly laid claim to the treasures which were being withheld from him. Antonius evaded or disallowed the claim: there was no money, he said, forthcoming; the money was not Cæsar's, but the state's; but for his own ingenuity all Cæsar's fortune would have been forfeited and his acts annulled. Octavius was thus thrown upon his own resources. He sold all he had, he borrowed of his friends and kinsmen, and effected the discharge of his public obligations. From that moment he assumed a position of authority and power. He had gained the people to his side; he had convinced politicians of his ability and force of character Antonius now felt that he had to reckon with no mean antagonist, and must determine whether to deal with him as a friend or an enemy. The liberators might give him less uneasiness, for their counsels were vacillating and timid; there was none among them who could take a decided step for the maintenance of the republic. Cicero, though spirited in tone and patriotic in sentiment, was wholly without power either himself to lead or to breathe animation into his associates. The chief men among them occupied themselves with their private enterprises, of no general interest to their cause. Decimus led his troops against the barbarians in the valleys of the Alps. Cassius withdrew into Syria, to seize the command there before his legitimate time of office. Sextus Pompeius made descents upon various points in the western Mediterranean, intent apparently on indiscriminate plunder. Brutus quitted Rome, but lingered on the coast of Campania, whence he gave directions for the prætorial shows which he dared not attend in person. At a later period he made up his mind to anticipate his term of government in Macedonia; but by the time he had crossed the Adriatic, Antonius had already secured the bulk of Cæsar's legions in that quarter. The senators already regarded him as their master. When one of their number, Calpurnius Piso, ventured to inveigh against him, his revilings passed unheeded; though eminent in rank he had no personal character to support them. Cicero, who had fled reluctantly from Italy, still kept in sight of the shore he loved, and when driven by the weather to come to land in Calabria, refused again to embark, and turned, with mournful presentiments, toward Rome.

Cicero declaims against Antonius.
U.C. 710. B.C. 44.

The consul had convoked the senate for September 1. Cicero had entered the city the day before, and was gratified by his favorable reception. Like other statesmen of his time, he never took account of the excessive instability of the Italian populace. He shrank, however, from attending the sitting of the senate. Supplications were to be voted; the dead Cæsar was to be enrolled among the national divinities. Antonius was present, and soon took advantage of the patriot's absence. The enmity between the two seems to have been instinctive and deep-seated. Cicero had been once banished and his house on the Palatine demolished. Antonius threatened to repeat the injury; but his menaces might be regarded perhaps as mere noisy declamations, and made little impression. The consul carelessly quitted the city to indulge in his licentious orgies at his Tiburtine villa, when Cicero seized the occasion to take his own place among the senators, and inveigh in set terms against the adversary who was in his turn absent. These sham duels of the Roman orators, not unfrequently recurring, may raise a smile; but in the present instance they have preserved for us some of the most stirring specimens of Roman eloquence. The insults of Antonius had stung Cicero to the quick, and he retorted with the weapon which he found most convenient. First he vindicated his own conduct both in leaving the city and in returning to it. While he refrained from any allusion to the tyrannicide, he analyzed the subsequent proceedings of Antonius, and exposed his abuse of Cæsar's papers, the posthumous demands he had advanced, the resolutions he had carried through the comitia of the tribes in defiance of the senate itself. He had recalled whom he would from banishment, made what laws he pleased, appointed his own creatures to office, and pleaded the will of the tyrant for every act of his own selfish and venal policy. The senate, not less unstable than the populace, warmed into admiration, and seemed for a moment to respond to the enthusiasm of the orator. Antonius himself was roused to fury, and hastened back to Rome to make his reply in the curia. Cicero was more afraid, perhaps, of his violence than of his arguments; his friends at least persuaded him to avoid a personal collision, and as the one entered the city the other withdrew into Campania. The senate seems to have listened obsequiously to whichever in turn claimed its attention.

CHAPTER X.
(U.C. 710. B.C. 44.—U.C. 712. B.C. 42)

THE SECOND TRIUMVIRATE: OCTAVIUS, ANTONIUS, AND LEPIDUS.

Octavius ingratiates himself with the soldiers.
Oct. B.C. 44

WHILE this war of words was raging, Octavius was silently undermining the consul's power with more effective weapons. With largesses and promises he was seducing the soldiers from his rival's standards. Antonius learnt with alarm that the troops which he had himself transported to Brundisium were falling under the influence of the young Cæsar's emissaries. On October 3 he departed in haste to stay their defection. At the same moment Octavius also quitted Rome, and visited the colonies which Cæsar had planted in Campania, Umbria, and the Cisalpine. He called the veterans to arms in the name of their beloved captain, and collected among them a force of 10,000 men. At the same time the heir of the tyrant and usurper was worming himself into the confidence of the unhappy patriot Cicero, who was eager to catch at any hope of support; and through him he worked upon the main body of the senate. To Cicero he addressed himself in frequent letters, praying him to return to Rome and once more save the state. He promised him regard, admiration, reverence; he loaded him with compliments and caresses; he called him father.

General preparations for war in the north of Italy.

Antonius felt that the time was come for vigorous action; the "young stripling" was an enemy not unworthy of his utmost exertions. He hastened to Ariminum to check the insubordination of the troops then quartered on the frontier of the Cisalpine. He rebuked them for the leaning they had shown to his rival; he offered them a donative. But he had fallen short of the spirit of the times; while he promised 400 sesterces, the captain of the future had assured them of 2,000 a-piece. Antonius was, however, still master of the ancient instruments of discipline. He smote their centurions with the axe, to the number of 300, if we may believe the furious declamations of Cicero, while his imperious consort, Fulvia, stood by and stimulated his vengeance. Upon the orator's tirades no reliance can be placed; but it seems that, by whatever means, Antonius brought some battalions together, and repaired with them, as a body guard, to Rome. On his arrival he summoned the senate to hear his charge against Octavius, of raising troops without official authority; for the youthful adventurer was invested with no magistracy. At the same moment, however, he learnt that two of his own legions had gone over to his enemy, and that the city could be held against him. There was no place for the consul in the senate house or the forum. He must retire to a distance and organize his resources, as Sulla and Marius, Cæsar and Pompeius, had each done in turn. He had given himself the government of the Cisalpine for the year which was about to begin. His first duty as legitimate proconsul would be to drive out Decimus Brutus, whose commission to the same government he declared to be by authority cancelled. He assumed the character of a defender of the republic, and summoned the pretender, who was already on the spot, to withdraw. When he arrived at Ariminum his forces amounted to four legions. Lepidus, who professed to act in concert with him, was advancing from Spain with four more. Pollio was still beyond the Pyrenees with three others, and Plancus, in the Further Gaul, had under him an equal number. These were the forces on which Antonius deemed that he might rely in his contest with the party of the liberators. But these legions were still widely separated; the soldiers were disloyal or indifferent, and their leaders had each his own private ends to serve. Decimus, from his central position, might intrigue with one or other of them, and cut them off from mutual support. But Octavius was now a military power also, having himself raised or detached from Antonius as many as five legions. Though possessed of no magistracy, and therefore of no legal imperium, still citizens of all classes thronged about him from various causes, and placed themselves at his disposal. He addressed the senate with a well-toned manifesto, which immediately recommended him to them as their true champion. Stationing himself at Arretium, so as to cover the capital from the attacks of every other competitor, he awaited the commencement of hostilities in the north of Italy, prepared himself to side with either party, or fall upon the survivor of the strife as circumstances might direct.

Cicero's political activity.—The Second Philippic. Dec., B.C. 44.

Such were the complications of this triple contest at the end of November in this fatal year. Cicero, whose courage had revived, was working with restless activity among the senators and citizens at home, striving to consolidate all parties against Antonius. He exhorted Decimus; he caressed Octavius. Doubtless, his real disposition inclined to the faction of the liberators, and he might think Decimus the ablest and not the least honest of the number. He could not fail to regard with dislike the nephew and heir of Cæsar; but he had been partly won by his dissimulation, and he was content to make use of him as an ally, in full belief that he would either fall from his own weakness, or easily succumb to the superior statecraft of a politician so experienced as himself. He engaged the senate to bestow its honors upon Octavius and give him military command; but he trusted much more to the loyalty of the consuls elect, Hirtius and Pansa, to raise a force to direct and control him, until the time when the heads of the republican party, Brutus and Cassius, Trebonius and Cimber, might be in a position to return to the West with overwhelming armies. Meantime, his efforts were chiefly concentrated on crushing Antonius. The moment had arrived for the publication of the Second Philippic, an harangue never delivered by word of mouth, but sent abroad as a written pamphlet, after being submitted to the inspection of private friends, and polished to the keenest edge by repeated touches from the great master himself. It was the pride of Cicero to compare himself to Demosthenes, the orator and the patriot, and to represent himself as contending against the enemy of Rome, as the Athenian had held in check the invader of Greece. The speech was consummate as a political instrument as well as a rhetorical composition. It spoke in decided language, branding Cæsar as a despot, but Antonius as a monster of iniquity. The author himself it represented as the stay of the commonwealth, the general object of hatred to every enemy of his country. It called on the citizens to arm with frantic earnestness. The effect corresponded to the energy of the blow. The picture drawn of Antonius struck the people with horror. The senate was at last moved with courage to defy him. The consuls, though personally attached to him, were fixed at once in the interests of the republic by the applause which hailed this stirring proclamation of its wrongs. Cicero, not unjustly elated by the shouts which echoed around him, believed himself now the mediator between all parties, the actual chief of the commonwealth. It was the no blest as well as the purest triumph of any Roman since the days of Camillus or Africanus. It was the just reward of so many years of self-devotion; and all our painful sense of the weaknesses by which that career had been disfigured, and which even at this moment marred its splendor, may fairly give way to the pleasure of contemplating it.

The Consuls Hirtius and Pansa take the field.
U.C. 711. B.C. 43.

But Antonius replied to words by deeds. He had quietly taken the field, and confined Decimus to the walls of Mutina. Cicero urged the senate, and the senate, at his behest, urged Octavius to attack him; but while he yet abstained from active measures, the friends of Antonius pleaded for forbearance, and the new consuls made yet another effort to preserve peace. Envoys were sent, negotiations were opened, but all failed. Cicero was loud and furious, and was sustained by the favorable accounts which he received from Brutus and Cassius, and the prospect of aid from Sextus. His influence proved effectual. Early in the year 43 Hirtius quitted the city and joined his consular army to the force of Octavius. Pansa reached them in the spring with fresh levies. In the absence of both the consuls, Cicero was allowed and encouraged to take the helm of the commonwealth. He poured forth in rapid succession his animated harangues against the public enemy; he breathed confidence into the desponding, and redoubled the efforts of the valiant. Clothed in the garb of war he traversed the streets, calling for contributions to the common cause, and filling the treasury with fines demanded from the malcontents. At the same time he maintained an active correspondence with the chiefs in the provinces, assured each in turn of the constancy of all the others, and bruited far and wide the high spirit of the veterans, the devotion of the people, the fidelity of the generals, and their abundant resources. Yet to the last the senate declined to recognise in these movements a state of civil war. Even when they charged Octavius and the consuls to raise the siege of Mutina, they would only characterize the contest as a "Gallic tumult," or a threatened outbreak of the national enemy beyond the Rubicon.

Both the consuls fall before Mutina.
April, B.C. 43.

On the approach of Hirtius and Octavius Antonius, the assailant of Decimus, broke up from his lines before Mutina, and advanced towards them. He still pretended, indeed, to negotiate; but when Pansa moved to effect a junction with them, he suddenly turned round, defeated, and mortally wounded him. Hirtius, however, was at hand to save the routed force from destruction, and he gave battle to the conqueror a few days later, with the support of Octavius. In this encounter the Antonians were, in their turn, driven into their camp; but the victorious Hirtius fell in the engagement, and thus both the consuls, by an unprecedented fatality, were stricken down at the same moment. The Romans, it would seem, could not believe that such a strange event was mere chance-medley. The rumor ran that Octavius had pierced Hirtius in the back with his own hand—a very unlikely circumstance; that he had engaged a surgeon to rub poison into Pansa's wound—a crime in itself less improbable, but on the other hand, one which it was only too easy to impute without the possibility of disproving it. The student of Roman history will remark that from this time the insinuation of secret assassination becomes more and more an ordinary weapon of political hostility, and he will put himself on his guard against it. Meanwhile the citizens, high and low, forgot, in their rejoicings at the victory, the disaster which had attended it. They carried Cicero to the capital with the loudest acclamations. He it was that had urged them to the war; in him they recognised the true victor of the field of Mutina. They believed the contest to be at an end. Decimus, they were assured, had issued from his walls, and was pursuing the routed Antonians towards the Alps. Plancus, confirmed in his loyalty to the republic, was doubtless descending from the North, and blocking the passes into Gaul. At the same moment some successes of Cassius against Dolabella in the East, the progress of Brutus in Macedonia, and the rumored approach of Sextus by sea, all concurred to increase their confidence.

Antonius unites with Lepidus and Plancus.

Before he expired, Pansa, it was said, had called Octavius to his bedside, and advertised him of the hatred which the senate really bore him, and of the treachery which they meditated. He assured him that, after all, his only chance of safety lay in a prompt reconciliation with the enemy whom he had just beaten. Nor was the crafty aspirant unprepared for such counsels. He had already arranged for a quarrel with Decimus, and had declared that the murder of his father, Cæsar, should never be forgiven. He now let Antonius understand that he had no desire to crush his father's friend. He refrained from preventing the junction which he was about to make with Lepidus beyond the Po. Antonius himself was evincing the courage and fortitude under adverse circumstances, for which, voluptuary though he was, he obtained high credit among his countrymen. He was "a powerful example," says Plutarch "to his soldiers, for though he was fresh from the enjoyment of so much luxury and expense, he drank foul water without complaining, and ate wild fruits and roots." He induced them in their flight to feed with him on the bark of trees and on the flesh of strange animals. Fortune seconded his energy. Plancus terminated his long in decision by throwing himself into the arms of the party which now, since the junction with Lepidus and the encouragement shown by Octavius, was manifestly the stronger. Antonius found himself at the head of twenty three legions.

Octavius demands the consulship.
Sept. B.C. 43.

This was the dreadful fact to which the senate now awoke from their dream of easy triumph. While expecting the arrival of Brutus and Cassius with overwhelming armies, they had sought to amuse their younger champion, and at the same time to corrupt his soldiers. Cicero was himself prepared to cast away the broken instrument of his successful policy. The senate, which had procured Octavius his election to the prætorship, now refused him the dignity of consul. Four hundred of his veterans came in a body to Rome to press his claim. The senate still refused, and he crossed the Rubicon at the head of eight legions. The senate forbade him to approach within ninety miles of the city. At the same time, however, they yielded to his demand, and offered a donative to his soldiers. But it was now too late. The bold adventurer had determined on his course, and did not halt till he reached the gates. The senators were appalled at this unlocked-for resolution. While putting forth a feeble show of defence, they slipped one by one into the intruder's camp. Cicero, indeed, was more constant than any but, he, too, yielded at last to the current, and presented himself before Octavius. He was received with taunts for his slackness. His fears were awakened; perhaps his conscience smote him. He might remember that he had himself urged with grim levity that the young candidate should be "smothered" with honors; and the next night he made his escape. The people, hastily assembled, pretended to elect Octavius to the consulship, and gave him a kinsman, named Pedius, for his colleague. This was September 22; on the following day he completed his twentieth year. The remnant of the senators—for many had disappeared—loaded him with flatteries and honors. They issued an empty command that Decimus should surrender to him his forces. Octavius directed the murderers of Cæsar to be cited before the public tribunals. Judgment passed against them by default, and they were interdicted fire and water.

Flight and death of Decimus Brutus.

The helpless upstart of the year before was now actually at the head of affairs, and could offer his own terms to whichever of the contending parties he should choose for his ally. While causing the hasty decrees of the senate against Antonius and Lepidus to be rescinded, he made them overtures which were readily accepted. Placed between these two chiefs and their respective powers, abandoned by Plancus, receiving no support from Octavius and the government at Rome, Decimus was lost. His troops, which had been easily levied, not less easily deserted him; the old military devotion to the general was utterly forgotten, even among the followers of a republican standard. With a few horsemen he attempted to break away into Macedonia, through the passes of the Rhætian Alps; but he was baffled by the mountaineers, and was delivered by a chief named Camelus into the hands of Antonius, by whom he was put to death. The blood of the tyrannicide cemented the alliance between the friend and the heir of the tyrant.

The Second Triumvirate.
U.C. 711. B.C. 43.

Towards the end of October, the Cæsarian leaders, Antonius, Lepidus, and Octavius, each at the head of independent if not of equal forces, met near Bononia, on an islet in the broad channel of a shallow stream called the Rhenus, and there deliberated on the fate of the vanquished and the partition of the common spoil. It was arranged between them, after three days' parley, that Octavius should resign the consulship in favor of Ventidius, a rude but trusty officer of the Antonian army, while the three superior chiefs should reign in partnership together over the city, the consuls, and the laws. They claimed the "consular power," without the official title, in common for a period of five years, with the right of appointing to all the magistracies. Their decrees were to have the force of law, without requiring the confirmation of the senate or the people. To this extraordinary commission, if we may so entitle a usurpation to which no other power but themselves was a party, they gave the name of a Triumvirate, or board of three, for constituting the commonwealth. The appointment of boards similarly designated for special purposes was an arrangement well known to the Roman constitution. The Quindecemvirs, the Septemvirs, and the Sevirs were each a permanent college for the discharge of certain sacred functions. The Decemvirs of famous memory had been specially charged with the settlement of the civil law of the state, and with its temporary government while that settlement was pending. All of these had emanated directly from the suffrage of the people, and held their powers subject to the popular will. But the Triumvirate now established owned no such popular origin, and bore no such elective character. It was an open and wilful usurpation; it was a "provisional government," as we might now call it, self-appointed in the first instance, standing upon its own basis, propped by an armed force, holding out, indeed, a prospect of self-surrender at some future time, but prepared meanwhile to assert its own arbitrary authority, and require universal obedience to it. The so-called Triumvirate of Cæsar, Pompeius, and Crassus had made no such public or patent assertion of conjoint power. The earlier Triumvirs obtained the title rather as a nickname than as indicating an established fact. They held similar power to that of their successors, but they put forth no actual profession of it. The idea of a Roman Tyranny had made great advances in the popular mind during the fifteen years which had intervened. It was the partition of absolute power between three, instead of its concentration in the hands of a single chief, that constituted the only essential difference between the despotism of the Triumvirs and the despotism of a king. The promise to resign the appointment at the end of five years was perceived to be merely illusory; the only hope the citizens could entertain of its fulfilment lay in the dissension which might be expected to prevail between the three co-equal occupants. And so it was that the alliance of the Triumvirs came indeed to a rapid end; but the end, as might have been equally well foreseen, was not the restoration of the popular government, but the consolidation of an absolute monarchy.

Division of the provinces among the Triumvirs.

Meanwhile, according to the first partition made between them, the two Gauls fell to Antonius, the Spains, with the Narbonensis, to Lepidus, Africa and the islands of Sicily and Sardinia to Octavius. Italy itself, the seat of empire, the three were to retain in common, while the eastern provinces, now held by Brutus and Cassius, they left for future division, when the enemy should be expelled from them. Against this enemy war was to be at once declared. Octavius and Antonius, each with twenty legions, charged themselves with the conduct of the war, and agreed to leave Lepidus, the least ambitious and least stirring of the confederates, but a man of high position, great wealth, and wide connections, to maintain their combined interest in the city. The swordsmen who followed them with no public or patriotic principles, were merely held together by the hopes of plunder, or at best by the military instinct of confidence in their leaders. Ample gratuities were poured into their hands, and estates assigned them from the lands of eighteen of the cities of Italy. The war was to be carried beyond the limits of the peninsula; but it was the peninsula itself which suffered the first and, perhaps, the worst effects of civil dissension. The troops, however, were satisfied with their share in the common compact, and insisted that it should be ratified by the espousal of Octavius to the daughter whom Fulvia had borne to her first husband, the tribune Clodius.

The proscriptions.

The Triumvirs now addressed an order to Pedius at Rome for the slaughter of seventeen of their principal adversaries. The houses of these selected victims were attacked at night, and most of them had fallen before their condemnation was notified to the citizens. Pedius, a brave and honorable man, died from horror and disgust at the crime he was imperiously required to execute. Octavius, Antonius, and Lepidus then entered the city on three successive days, each attended by a single legion. The temples and towns were occupied by the troops; the banners of the conquerors waved in the Forum, and cast their ominous shadow over the heads of the assembled citizens. A plebiscitum was required to give a bare semblance of legality to an usurpation which had been already effected. On November 27, the triumvirate was proclaimed. The potentates about to quit Rome to combat the murderers of Cæsar in the East would leave no enemies in their rear. They decreed, not a massacre, such as Sulla's, but a formal proscription. Sitting with a list of chief citizens before them, each picked out the names of the victims he personally required. Each purchased the right to proscribe a kinsman of his colleagues by surrendering one of his own. The fatal memorial was headed with the names of a brother of Lepidus, an uncle of Antonius, and a cousin of Octavius. Again were enacted the brutal scenes which closed the civil wars of the last generation. Centurions and soldiers were dispatched in quest of the most important victims. The pursuit was joined by mercenary cut-throats and private enemies. Slaves attacked their masters, and debtors their creditors. The heads of the victims were affixed to the Rostra to certify the claims of the murderers, but the Triumvirs themselves did not always pause to identify them.

Death of Cicero. Dec. 7, B.C. 43.

The cold and unnatural cruelty of some of these assassinations has made them more peculiarly odious, even amidst the many butcheries of the Roman civil wars. It would seem, however, that the proscribed were not in all cases hotly pursued. Many crossed the sea to Macedonia, others into Africa; still more took refuge on board the vessels with which Sextus Pompeius was cruising off the coast of Italy. Some escaped by bribery when entreaty failed; and Octavius seems in some cases to have set his own leniency in contrast with the more brutal ferocity of his associates. But Antonius had demanded the death of Cicero, and Octavius, to the horror of all time, had consented. Nevertheless, some opportunity was given even to Cicero to effect his escape, and he was not overtaken till a month later. Marcus Cicero was at the moment with his brother Quintus at his Tusculan villa. On the first rumor of the proscription they fled and gained Astura, another of the orator's residences on a little island off Antium. From thence they proposed to embark for Macedonia. Quintus, indeed, was promptly seized and slain, but the surviving fugitive reached the sea, set sail, again landed, again embarked, and landed once more at Formiæ, worn out with distress of mind, and suffering from sickness. In vain was he warned of the danger of delay. "Let me die," he exclaimed, "in my fatherland, which I have so often saved." But his slaves now lifted him with gentle violence into his litter, and hurried him towards the coast. Scarcely had the house been quitted when an officer named Popilius, a client, it was said, whose life Cicero had saved, approached and thundered at the closed doors. A traitor pointed out the direction which the fugitive had taken, and Cicero had not yet reached the beach when he saw the pursuers gaining upon him. His own party were numerous, and would have fought in his defence, but he forbade them. He bade his slaves set down the litter, and with his eyes fixed steadily on his murderers, offered his throat to the sword. Some covered their faces with their hands, and their agitated leader drew his blade thrice across it before he could sever the head from the body. The bloody trophy was carried to Rome, and set up by Antonius in front of the Rostra. He openly exulted in the spectacle, and rewarded the assassins with profuse liberality. Fulvia, the wife of Antonius and the relict of Clodius, pierced, it is said, the tongue with a needle, in revenge for the sarcasms it had uttered against both her husbands.

Reflections on the death of Cicero.

In the circumstances both of his life and death Cicero has been compared to Demosthenes. Each struggled for his country against an enemy and a tyrant, and each was proscribed and hunted to death for the eloquence with which he had assailed him. Each battled for a cause which was really hopeless; for both Athens and Rome had forfeited the power of maintaining their own freedom, perhaps we may say the right to contend for it. But if the crimes of Roman society were more glaring than those of the Athenian, which was imbecile rather than furious, there were at least some great and noble characters in the senate who might dignify the struggle, however hopeless. Among the magnates of the city to whom Cicero introduces us in his letters and his speeches, there were men of virtue and honor, true lovers of their country, and admirers of patriotism such as his own. They lacked, perhaps, the genuine devotion of the older days; and, with the single exception, it may be said, of Cato, have left us no historic examples of public virtue. The best among them were no doubt most conscious of the false position in which they were placed by the corruption of their own adherents and the evil temper of the times; but the best of them were indeed among the weakest in character, and least capable of influencing the multitude around them. Cicero himself was not, except once or twice, and for a moment only, a real power in the state. But he has left as statesman an example of sincere patriotism, to which the lovers of public virtue may always point with exultation. To the last he never deserted his place as a citizen. He has enriched human history with the portrait which the gods were said to ad mire, of a good man struggling with adversity; and the respect in which his own countrymen held him, both in his own time and in later generations, is a redeeming feature in the hard and selfish character of the Roman people.

Settlement of the Triumvirs' government at Rome. B.C. 42.

Such were the atrocities and horrors with which the year (B.C. 43) closed. Lepidus and Plancus, who next entered on the consulship, commanded the people, still full of dismay and mourning, to celebrate the commencement of their reign with mirth and festivity. They demanded the honor of a triumph for victories, about which our annals are silent, in Gaul and Spain. Both the one and the other had sacrificed their own brother in the proscription; and when the fratricides passed along in their chariots, the soldiers, it is said, with the usual camp license, chanted, as they followed, "The consuls triumph, not over the Gauls, but the Germans," i. e. their brothers. The massacres had now ended, but a course of confiscation commenced. All the inhabitants of Rome and Italy were required to lend a tenth of their fortunes, and to give the whole of one year's income. The consuls proposed an oath to the citizens to maintain all Cæsar's enactments, and they proceeded to accord to him divine honors, by an Oriental fiction unknown at least to the Romans since the legendary days of Romulus. The Triumvirs followed their hero's example in assigning all the chief magistracies for several years in advance. Octavius undertook to drive Sextus out of Sicily, where he had established himself under the protection of a flotilla manned by pirates and adventurers; but the passage of the narrow straits was too strictly guarded. Antonius crossed without delay to the coast of Epirus.

CHAPTER XI.
(U.C. 712. B.C. 42.)

LAST EFFORT OF THE REPUBLICANS: THE BATTLE OF PHILIPPI.

Independence of the Roman armies in the East.

THE conduct of the struggle which was now about to open, affords an instructive view of the condition of the Roman dominion in the last days of the victorious commonwealth. We have seen the alacrity with which Cassius, the chief military leader of the republican party, hastened to throw himself into the remote East and assume the government of the Syrian province. He found himself there at the head of a large army, supported by levies from many states and tributary potentates, sustained by the unbounded resources of the wealthiest region of the known world, constituting an independent power but slightly connected in political feeling with Rome itself, and long disused to the restraints of civil law; an army encamped upon a subject territory on which it claimed to live at free quarters. The only rule which it acknowledged was that of its own commander, and this rule it obeyed only so far as he gratified its appetite for plunder and its ordinary contempt of discipline. The great army of the East would follow its leader to any enterprise of conquest among the wealthy regions of Asia, but it did not care to cross the seas and encounter the defenders of the poorer realms of Europe. It preferred the sack of cities and temples to an assignment of lands, and it was dimly conscious that on the soil of Italy its victories could not be crowned by the pillage of Rome, nor even that of Capua or Naples. The veterans of Sulla and Pompeius must be content, when they transferred themselves from the East to the shores of Italy, with the tardy acquisition of forfeited estates and the position of military colonists. Accordingly, the forces of Cassius were all-powerful at Antioch or Ephesus; but they were of little avail for the recon quest of the western world.

Roman society at Athens.

Brutus, as we have seen, had been more loth to quit Rome. His patriotic spirit was attached, like that of Cicero, to the home and centre of his nation, and could ill brook the prospect of a long and, perhaps, a final separation from it. But he too, as a student of Hellenic culture, was attracted to the East, as far at least as Greece and Athens, by its scholastic associations; and the command which he had secured for himself in Macedonia brought him into direct contact with the men of thought and learning who still congregated from all parts, and especially from Rome herself, in the schools of the Porch, the Garden, and the Academy. Athens was at this time much frequented by the young nobility of Italy; many who came in their tender years for the purpose of study conceived a special attachment to the place, which weaned them from their own country, and made Greece a second home to them. The Romans in Greece constituted a provincial society which owned but a languid allegiance to their native city, and cared, perhaps, little for their natural connection with it. Among the youthful students of the Athenian university, if we may so entitle it, Brutus enlisted many gallant spirits, such as the young poet Horace, who were fired by the name of liberty, but were more ready to defend themselves in their adopted country against an invader from the West than to make any attempt to recover a footing on the shores which they had virtually abandoned.

The natural repulsion of the East from the West.

If we may compare this state of things with an instance from modern history, the Romans at this period in the East were in some marked respects not unlike the people of the Southern States of North America. Desirous as they were chiefly of being left alone in the enjoyment of their peculiar advantages, the Romans of the West, like the northerners of the transatlantic continent, would not suffer them to depart, being determined that the empire should not be divided, and that the wealthiest portion of their dominions should not be wrested from the common centre. Doubtless, if there was much patriotism in this determination, there was at the same time much greed of power. But so it was that the government installed at Rome would never consent to the separation of the East from the West. The Cæsarians would not suffer such a separation to be effected by the Pompeians, who for their part might not be unwilling to acquiesce in it. The followers of the triumvirs would not concede it to the republicans, who, in their turn, would have made little effort to oppose it; and again at the next turn of fortune to which we shall be directed we shall find the triumvir who is master of the West inexorable in his resolution to recover the eastern half of the empire from his rival beyond the Ægean. It was, in fact, with the utmost difficulty that at three successive crises the unity of the whole unwieldy mass was preserved, and at last so firmly welded together by Augustus and Agrippa that it endured without a rapture, though not without some violent shocks, for nearly four centuries. To the last, however, the union was mechanical, so to say, rather than organic. There was no community of interest, no homogeneous feeling; no moral fusion between the East and the West; the two hemispheres were maintained in political union only, as they had been first compacted, by the firm will and strong hand of Rome.

Meeting of Brutus and Cassius at Sardis.

The horrible condition to which the civil wars had reduced the long flourishing communities of the East appears in a way in which the Roman chiefs in that quarter were obliged to maintain their armies. As soon as Antonius threatened them with an attack, it became necessary to arm and move the vast hosts which could be easily raised to confront him, the most forcible measures were demanded to supply the means required. This want of means would have prevented any aggressive movement even had the liberators and those that followed them really cared to carry the war into Italy. But, in fact, they could not attempt to do so. The legionaries themselves might have refused to engage in a bloody and unprofitable campaign while the cities of the East offered them abundant gratifications. They found or provoked petty enemies around them, and compelled their chiefs to lead them against the Lycians, the Rhodians, and the Cappadocians, either for pay or plunder. Brutus himself consented to the sack of Xanthus, where the wretched people threw themselves into the flames of their own city. Cassius wantonly attacked the great emporium of Rhodes, mulcted it of 8,500 talents, and enforced the fine by cutting off the heads of fifty of its principal citizens. The whole province of Asia was subjected to the severest proscriptions of which these are perhaps only specimens. At last Brutus, hardly less guilty than his colleagues, but more sensitive to the sin and scandal, interfered to restrain such disgraceful cruelties. At Sardis, where the two proconsuls met to arrange their plan of operations, he sharply rebuked Cassius for bringing odium on their common cause; but Cassius pleaded his inability to restrain his mercenaries, and Brutus let the matter pass with a few unavailing murmurs.

The battle of Philippi, Nov. B.C. 42. U.C. 712.—Death of Cassius.

The character of Brutus as a dreamy enthusiast is marked by the venerable legend of a terrible figure that appeared to him at night and announced itself as his evil demon, which should present itself to him again at Philippi. It was reported further that Brutus divulged the ominous vision to Cassius, the Epicurean, who explained to him the reasoning by which his master in philosophy had demonstrated the vanity of apparitions. Nevertheless, the Stoic idealist continued anxious and dissatisfied. When at last the republican forces mustered in Macedonia, in the vicinity of Philippi, 100,000 strong, and prepared to encounter the armies, still more numerous, of the triumvirs, the vision, it is said, recurred; the demon was faithful to his appointment. Never were men's eyes and ears more open to bodings of evil than at this disturbed crisis of human history. The ghosts of Marius and Sulla were supposed to have betokened the renewal of the civil wars. The disaster of Carrhæ had been preceded by adverse omens. The battle of Pharsalia had been announced hundreds of miles away at the moment of the impious struggle. Presages of dire significance had been noticed before that fell encounter; similar intimations, it would seem, could not be wanting to the last fatal scene which was now about to open. Brutus and Cassius posted themselves on two eminences about twelve miles east of Philippi, their left covered by the sea, from which they drew their supplies. Antonius placed his camp opposite to that of Cassius; Octavius, on his left, faced the army of Brutus. Cassius, it is said, aware of the enemy's lack of provisions, would have refrained from action; but Brutus, ever fretful and impatient, overruled his wiser counsels.

The contest between forces so numerous extended over a wide space, and was conducted with little mutual concert between the commanders on either side. Octavius was sick and could not take part in the encounter. More than once in the course of his career did he suffer these untoward hindrances, upon which his enemies did not fail to comment; and now his division was overpowered and precipitately pursued. Brutus believed the battle won; but in the meanwhile Antonius had charged, with no less success, on the right; Cassius had been driven from his camp, and descrying, when left almost alone, a body of horsemen advancing, had rashly concluded that they were enemies in pursuit, and had thrown himself upon the sword of a freedman. The scouts of Brutus, sent to advertise him of his colleague's advantage, arrived a moment too late.

Second battle, and death of Brutus.

The effect of this blunder was disastrous. Cassius had exercised some control over the soldiers, but Brutus was utterly powerless with them. In vain did he scatter all his treasures among them; they called out the louder for more. In vain did he yield up his prisoners to their cruelty; they grew even more vindictive and bloodthirsty. He was compelled to promise them the plunder of Thessalonica in order to retain them yet awhile at his standard; for the Cæsarians were reduced to great straits, and the dispersion of their fleet on the same day as the recent battle rendered their advanced position no longer tenable. Both the armies still kept the ground which they had before occupied. Twenty days after the first engagement Brutus was hurried into renewing it. The field was well contested; the instinct of fighting was equally keen on both sides, though on neither was there any real principle at stake, nor any definite object in view. The Roman legionary had become nothing more than a gladiator, bold, expert, and desperate. At the end of the day the Cæsarians had broken the ranks of their adversaries, and Octavius assailed them in their camp. Brutus, with four legions kept a position through the night on the neighboring hills. The next day his men refused to fight, and he could only secure, with a few attendants, some hours of concealment, after which he terminated his life with a blow of his own sword, when none of them could be induced to do him the last faithful service.

The end of the Roman republic.

The cause of the republic is said to have perished on the field of Philippi; but, to speak truly, the republic itself had, as we have seen, perished already. The fragments of the broken party which had seemed to gather round it collapsed under this final blow. Many nobles and officers who survived the carnage were captured in the flight, or surrendered themselves to the victors, who treated them, strange to say, with distinguished clemency. A remnant was taken off by their own fleet, and sought refuge with Sextus at the head of his piratical armament. The Cæsarian leaders had shown themselves abler than their opponents. A curse of weakness and barrenness seemed to cling to the murderers of the great dictator, who proved themselves incompetent throughout to originate any bold design, to overcome any difficulties, or to engender even the slightest enthusiasm for the phantom which they followed. Brutus, the best, but, perhaps, the weakest, of the whole crew, died muttering a spiritless verse which rails at virtue as an empty name and no better than a slave to fortune. If so it be, he should surely have bethought himself thereof before he gratified his spite or vanity by the crime of an assassination. Amidst the fury, indeed, of armed factions it was plain that the government of the world had passed out of the hands of contemplative and philosophic students, if such could have ever hoped to retain it. The strong man was the only man who could rule, and the strong man was more than ever necessary to prevent the world from sinking into anarchy. The true patriot at that moment would have hailed the advent of any ruler vigorous enough to control events, and might have forgiven him an act of usurpation in which lay the only chance of progress or at least of peace for the future. But the vain idea that the republic was possible now passed out of men's minds, never again to be revived, except casually and for a moment in the imagination of hot-headed and feeble enthusiasts. There yet remained a short struggle between the personal claims of the foremost captains of the day; but the commonwealth in general might await with some calmness the issue, which could only be the establishment of a constituted government under the form of monarchy. From the republic to the empire might be a moral decline, but it was plainly both natural and inevitable.

CHAPTER XII.
U.C. 712. B.C. 42.—U.C. 724. B.C. 30.

Contest Between Octavius and Antonius.—Battle of Actium.—Octavius Becomes Master of the State.

Further division of the provinces.
U.C. 712. B.C. 42.

The two triumvirs who had conducted the campaign against the common enemy paid little regard to the colleague whom they had left in empty state behind them. After Philippi they arranged a new division of the provinces, Antonius taking Gaul and Illyricum, Octavius seizing upon Spain and Numidia, and retaining Italy with the Cisalpine in common between the two, while to Lepidus they gave at first no province at all, though at a later period they allowed him to hold the small but important district of Africa. This partition of the provinces seems to have been made in order to allow each chief to gratify his particular followers with subordinate appointments; but the real distribution of power was of a different kind. Octavius returned to Rome and became at once supreme throughout the West, while Antonius preferred to remain in the opposite quarter, and reign over its wealthy regions and luxurious cities, which were all placed in subjection to him. While Octavius devoted himself in Italy to the interests of his veterans, his colleague lavished upon himself and his parasites all the spoils he could accumulate. His arrival was everywhere regarded with the utmost dread by cities and potentates, and his favor purchased by flatteries and presents.

Cleopatra's conquest of Antonius.

The Clever and artful Cleopatra addressed him, however, in another fashion. The death of her admirer, Cæsar, exposed her to imminent perils at

Alexandria, both from within and from without. It was essential to her security to gain the protection of the new ruler of the East. Antonius had seen her in the train of his master, and even then, no doubt, he had been struck by her showy fascinations. She had returned to Egypt to secure her throne there; but he now required her to meet him in Cilicia, and answer for some imputed intrigues with his enemy Cassius. The queen was confident in her charms, which had already proved so powerful. Instead of appearing herself as a suppliant, she meant to bring him on his knees before her; and she succeeded. Steering for Tarsus for the interview demanded of her, she sailed up the Cydnus in a gilded vessel, with purple sails and silver oars, to the sound of Oriental music. She was seen reclining under a spangled canopy in the garb of Venus, surrounded by Cupids, Graces, and Nereids. Antonius himself had jovially assumed the attributes of Bacchus. The astonished natives hailed the happy conjunction of the two most genial of their divinities. Dazzled by her splendid equipage, he invited her to land and sit at banquet with him but she haughtily replied that he must come and attend upon herself. The first interview sealed his fate. For the rude triumvir, more of a gladiator than a statesman, Cleopatra discarded the Grecian elegance of manners which had charmed the polished dictator; she sat through his tipsy orgies, laughed at his camp jokes, delighted him with her own saucy sallies, and so maintained the hold which she at once acquired over him, till she first ruined and finally betrayed him.

War of Perusia.

While, however, Antonius was forgetting wife and country, and postponing the war announced against the Parthians for the sake of his new plaything, his brother Lucius had joined with Fulvia in a wanton attack upon Octavius in Italy. Lucius Antonius and Servilius had occupied the consulship for the year 41. Fulvia, daring and ambitious, ruled them both, while the indolent Lepidus fell altogether under eclipse. The return of Octavius surprised and alarmed the guilty confederates. Fulvia was irritated by his dismissal of her daughter Claudia, whom he had but just wedded to satisfy the soldiers. She was mortified also at her husband's desertion, and hoped to tear him away from Alexandria by raising commotions at home. With these views she fomented the discontent of the Italian proprietors, whose lands Octavius had assigned to his veterans, many of whom had already seized their arms to defend themselves, while the veterans themselves were murmuring at the discontent which their victims so naturally manifested. The young triumvir was reduced to great straits. He exerted himself to pacify his followers with fresh confiscations; but his friend, M. Agrippa, shut up Lucius in Perusia, and at last reduced him to capitulation by stress of hunger. It is said that Octavius caused 300 knights and senators to be sacrificed to the shade of his father; but the story of the *Aræ Perusinæ* seems little credible, though doubtless his brutal soldiery thirsted for blood, and perhaps he gratified them too largely. We learn, however, that at all events he spared L. Antonius, and even gave him an appointment in Spain.

A third partition of the empire.

Antonius was now roused to exertion, and for a moment he broke away from the toils of his Egyptian paramour. He sent his lieutenant, Ventidius, to make head against the Parthians, whose hostility, ever ready to kindle in arms, he had already challenged; but he shaped his own course for the West. At Athens he met his consort, Fulvia, who upbraided him with his long abandonment of wife and friends but as he was exerting himself just then to repair his error, the rebuke was at least unseasonable, and his resentment seems to have crushed her spirit and hastened her end, which quickly followed. Relieved from this domestic embarrassment, he led his active squadrons to the coast of the Adriatic. There he made a compact with Sextus Pompeius, and got himself transported across the straits; but the plunder which he seems to have allowed raised the indignation of Italy and Rome, which had learnt to regard him as a foreign invader. In Sextus, his base associate, they had long ceased to recognize the son of their ancient favorite. The prince of the pirates had renounced, it was reported, the manners and principles of his countrymen, had affected to be the son of Neptune, and had actually forgotten the Latin language. Accordingly, when Octavius drew his sword to resist this invasion, the sympathies of the people were enlisted warmly on his side as the champion of the senate, the people, and the national divinities. The soldiers, however, were at this moment stronger than the people, and disposed of their chiefs at their will. They now compelled the two rival leaders to treat. A fresh partition of the Empire gave the East to Antonius, from the Adriatic to the Euphrates, where he was charged to control the Parthians; the West to Octavius, with the conduct of the war against Sextus. Africa was abandoned to Lepidus. Octavia, the sister of the young Cæsar, recently left a widow by Marcellus, married the widower Antonius. The rivals, thus outwardly reunited, hastened to Rome together, and celebrated their alliance with much hollow rejoicing.

The triumvirs concert terms with Sextus and again resort to arms against him.—Battle of Naulochus. U.C. 717. B.C. 37.

The treaty of Brundisium gave to each of the two contracting parties a new start in power, but it put no check upon their rivalry. The final issue of the long struggle between them, thus carefully balanced, must depend upon personal ability and fortune. The popularity which the younger had already acquired gave him a ground of vantage; but he had three arduous tasks before him—to keep Rome and Italy contented, to contend at the same time by sea against the resources and skill of Sextus, and to maintain by constant exercise the courage and ardor of his soldiers. In the first of these undertakings he was ably seconded by Cilnius Mæcenas, whom he made his chief administrator at home; who soothed rival ambitions in the senate and the forum, and pacified the murmurs of the dispossessed proprietors throughout the peninsula. His next endeavor was to come to terms with Sextus, with whom he had connected himself by an opportune marriage with his sister Scribonia. The son of the great Pompeius was now invited to confer with the triumvirs at Misenum, and the islands of Sicily, Sardinia, and Corsica were assigned to him as his share of empire. The allied potentates entertained one another at banquets in a vessel riding at sea, but moored to the land for the equal security of all; and Sextus gallantly declined, though not without an effort, to let his bold lieutenant, Mænas, cut the cable and carry off his rivals with him. But when he refused to restore some places he had taken on the coast of Italy, the western triumvir took up arms against him. In his naval enterprises Octavius was well supported by his friend Agrippa, who constructed the Julian port, on the Campanian coast, employed one year in equipping a powerful fleet, and, after some misadventures, effected his enemy's complete overthrow in the sea-fight of Naulochus, off the coast of Sicily. Sextus fled in confusion to the East, and was speedily crushed by Antonius, to whom he vainly looked for protection. Octavius had already repudiated Scribonia, and allied himself with the great houses of the republic by a curious love-marriage with Livia, divorced for his sake by her husband, Tiberius Claudius Nero.

Renewal of the triumvirate.
U.C. 717. B.C. 37.

The term prescribed for the triumvirate had expired on the last day of the year 38, but there had been many precedents for the protraction of such irregular powers, and the three colleagues were on sufficiently good terms with one another to agree to a renewal of their compact for another period of five years. The senate and the people submitted without an audible murmur to a tyranny which was now more autocratic than ever. Such, it seems, was the result of a meeting of Octavius and Antonius at Tarentum, in which they pretended to maintain a cordial alliance between themselves, while they retained their superiority over their feeble colleague.

Fall of Lepidus.
B.C. 36.

When Lepidus ventured at last to turn against the ruler of the West, Octavius easily put down so feeble a pretender, and spared the life of a magnate illustrious from his birth and from the dignity which he held of chief pontiff. The younger Cæsar had now learnt from the elder the policy of clemency, which he continued to practise to the end of his long career. He was cementing his power and popularity in every direction, with a view, no doubt, to the final struggle which he knew to be impending; and his last efforts were directed to keeping his troops in training by campaigns against the barbarians in Dalmatia, where neither spoil nor glory was to be acquired, but which now presented the only field for the arms of a western imperator.

Disastrous campaign of Antonius against the Parthians.
U.C. 718. B.C. 36.

On the other hand, a great sphere was open to the martial enterprise of the triumvir in the East. Antonius had acted loyally towards his colleague in supplying him with vessels for his contest with Sextus; at the same time he had required from him a contingent of 20,000 men for the expedition which he was preparing to conduct against the Parthians. Having secured this succor, however, he did not scruple to abandon the sister of Octavius, whom he had so recently espoused as a pledge of constant alliance, and rushed again into the toils of Cleopatra, with whom he indulged in sport and revelry till his armaments were completed. About mid-summer of the year B.C. 36, he had assembled 100,000 men on the Euphrates to follow up the partial successes of Ventidius. He had, indeed, delayed the advance too long; and from the haste with which he now moved he suffered his machines to fall into the rear, so that when he reached Praaspa, 300 miles beyond the Tigris, unopposed, he found himself destitute of the means for besieging a strong and well-defended city. An attempt to reduce it by blockade was baffled by the setting in of the cold season in the lofty regions into which he had unwarily plunged. He retreated, and suffered in his retreats hardships almost unparalleled, such as those which attended the flight of Napoleon from Moscow. On his crossing the Araxes, however, the Parthians at length desisted from their pursuit; but still intent on regaining the festive halls of Alexandria he hurried his weary soldiers along with great distress and loss. He rejoined the queen in Syria, whither she had advanced to meet him, and returned with her, defeated but unabashed, to the delights of her court in Egypt.

Impending rapture between the triumvirs.

So miserable a retreat after so rash an advance could be regarded only as a grave disaster. The base triumvir chose, however, to announce himself as a conqueror. Octavius did not care to contest his claim, and still affected to maintain a cordial understanding with him. Antonius had quitted Alexandria, bent upon another campaign in the East. Octavia, sent with specious compliments by her brother, had gone forward to meet him, bringing with her some picked battalions, well armed and clothed, with other valuable equipments for his army. She hoped even now to win him away from his disgraceful amour with the foreigner. Cleopatra was on the watch to baffle her endeavors. The queen soon succeeded in luring her lover back to Egypt; Octavia returned with dignity to Rome, at last abandoning her reckless lord to the fate which he merited. Antonius grew more and more insensible to the opinions of his countrymen. In the year following (B.C. 34) he made some inroads into Armenia, picked a quarrel with the king, Artavasdes, and carried him, loaded with golden chains, to Alexandria. For these successes be awarded himself a triumph, which he celebrated, to the disgust of all Roman citizens, in the streets of his barbaric capital.

Antonius amuses himself at Alexandria.
U.C. 721. B.C. 33.

The first months of the year 33 were passed at Alexandria amidst licentious orgies, the rumor of which caused much resentment at Rome, where they were no doubt depicted in the darkest colors. The aim of Cleopatra, it was urged, was to wean the Roman imperator from his national ideas; to make him a foreigner and an Egyptian like herself; to render it impossible for him to show himself again in Rome. This she might, perhaps, easily effect; but it was more difficult for her to keep the idle voluptuary constantly occupied and constantly amused. Her personal qualities were of the most varied kind, and such as we might suppose would have been lost upon a coarse debauchee like Antonius. She was an admirable singer and musician: she was skilled in many languages and possessed of high intellectual gifts, in addition to the lighter artifices of her sex. She pampered her lover's appetites and stimulated his flagging interest with ingenious surprises and playful ridicule, sending divers, as we read, to fasten a salted fish to the bait of his angling rod, and dissolving in a cup of vinegar a pearl of inestimable value. Painters and sculptors were charged to group the illustrious pair together, and the coins of the realm represented the effigies of the two conjointly. The Roman legionary bore the name of Cleopatra on his shield, like a Macedonian body-guard. Masques were represented at court, in which the versatile Plancus sank into the character of a stage buffoon, and enacted the part of the sea-god Glaucus, while the princely lovers arrayed themselves as the native divinities Isis and Osiris.

Preparations for a struggle.
U.C. 721. B.C. 33.

Meanwhile the senate had decreed Octavius a legitimate triumph for his successes over the Liburni and Iapydes. He had sustained an honorable wound, and had recovered his reputation for personal courage, on which some slur had been cast by his unseasonable sicknesses. But the youthful hero was not impatient for the celebration of his victory, and deferred the solemnity, while he kept the city in intense expectation of a national crisis by upbraiding Antonius with his foreign connection, and pointing to him as an enemy to the commonwealth. Antonius, on his part, had charges also to make against his colleague. These were personal indeed rather than patriotic. He complained that his just share of the spoils of Lepidus had been withheld from him; but such a complaint met with no response from the senate and people, and Octavius could well afford to disregard it. The Eastern chief began now to prepare in earnest for a final struggle. He had been collecting troops for another attack upon the Parthians. Towards the end of 33 B.C. he directed his forces westward, appointing Ephesus for the rendezvous of the contingents from many provinces and nations which he summoned to his standards. Greeks, Asiatics, and Africans found themselves arrayed around him. Cleopatra appeared herself at the head of the great Egyptian navy. Her galleys were renowned for their size and splendid equipment, and combined with the resources of the eastern Mediterranean to form the largest armament that had ever been launched on its waters, at least since the time of Xerxes.

The triumvirate expires and is not renewed.
U.C. 722. B.C. 32.

The consuls for the year 32 were Domitius Ahenobarbus and Sosius, both of them adherents of Antonius, who had received their office according to the agreement then still existing between him and his colleague. But this advantage was balanced by the defection of some of his chief supporters.

Plancus, who had consented to degrade himself for the amusement of his patron's court, now reappeared in the senate and denounced his treachery and frivolity. This man betrayed to Octavius the testament of the renegade imperator, which he had been charged to deposit with the vestal virgins, and in which, it seems, Antonius had acknowledged the validity of Cæsar's odious union with the foreigner, had declared her child Cæsario to be the dictator's legitimate son, had confirmed his own donations of crowns and provinces to his bastards, and, finally, had directed that his own body should be entombed by the side of Cleopatra's in the mausoleum of the Ptolemies. None could now doubt the rumors which prevailed, that he had pledged the queen in his cups to remove the government of the world to Alexandria, and prostrate the gods of the Capitol before the monstrous deities of the Nile. Octavius was at once greeted as the true champion of the nation, the maintainer of its principles and its faith. The consuls hurried away from the city, in which they found themselves ill at ease. Octavius, still moderate, still politic, refrained from declaring the impious chief a public enemy. He was content with proclaiming war against Egypt. The second term of the triumvirate had expired, and he did not renew it. He directed the senate to annul the appointment of Antonius to the next consulship, and assumed it himself with Messala for the year 31.

Forces assembled on the coast of Epirus.
U.C. 723. B.C. 31.

Even the handful of nobles who repaired at this crisis to the side of Antonius, now urged him to dismiss Cleopatra, and reduce the impending struggle to a personal contest with his rival. He replied by formally divorcing his legitimate consort, and thus breaking the last legal tie that bound him to his country. He had now assembled 100,000 foot and 12,000 horse. The kings of Mauretania, of Commagene, Paphlagonia, and Cilicia followed his banners. His fleet counted 500 large war-galleys, some of them with eight or even ten banks of oars. The forces of Octavius were somewhat inferior by land; his vessels were much fewer in number, but of a lighter and more manageable class. Antonius adopted Patræ, in the Peloponnesus, for his winter quarters, while he disposed of his vast armies, for their better support, along the coast of Epirus. But his navy suffered from sickness, and Agrippa contrived to throw the Cæsarian forces across the Adriatic. From that moment defection commenced. Domitius was the first to abscond; many princes of Asia followed his example. Antonius fancied himself surrounded by traitors he distrusted even Cleopatra, and required her to taste, in his company, all the viands that were set before him.

Battle of Actium.
U.C. 723. B.C. 31. (Sept. 2)

Some partial engagements first took place at sea, in which Agrippa's skill gained the advantage. Antonius was quickly discouraged. He would have withdrawn his land forces further into the interior; but Cleopatra, fearing for her own retreat, dissuaded him from this project. A strange story is related that he sent Octavius a challenge to single combat, which was scornfully rejected. Thereupon he made preparations for flight, and determined to lead a general attack on the Cæsarian fleet, with no hope of victory, but merely to gain an opportunity of escape. For several days the agitation of the sea would not allow either armament to move. At last, on September 2, the wind fell, the waters became smoother, and with the rise of a gentle breeze the Antonian galleys made for the open sea. Their huge hulks were ill-adapted for manœuvering, but they hurled massive stones from their wooden towers, and thrust forth ponderous irons to grapple the unwary assailant. The light triremes of Octavius were, on the other hand, both dexterous and agile. Their well-trained rowers bore up or backed with rapidity, and swept away the banks of the enemy's oars under cover of a shower of arrows. The combat was animated but indecisive; but while the Antonian barges rolled heavily on the water, incapable of attacking their puny assailants, suddenly Cleopatra's galley, moored in the rear, hoisted sail, and threaded the maze of combatants, followed by the Egyptian squadron of sixty vessels. Antonius was not unprepared for the signal. He leapt into a boat and hastened after her. The rage and shame of his adherents filled them with despair. Many tore down their turrets and threw them into the sea, to lighten their decks for flight; yet many continued to fight recklessly or blindly. Too lofty to be scaled, too powerful to be run down, their huge vessels were at last destroyed by fire.

Three hundred of them had been captured; few probably escaped. The land forces refused for a time to believe in their leader's ignominy, and might, perhaps, have still maintained their position; but when their commander, Canidius, abandoned the camp for the Cæsarian quarters, they offered no further resistance.

Octavius secures the fruits of his victory.

So complete a victory as that of Actium has seldom been so easily gained. The accounts we have received of the conduct of the miserable Antonius come, no doubt, from the side of the victors; but it is impossible to suppose that he lost so great a fleet and army so utterly, except by his own misconduct. Octavius might now feel himself secure, and proceed to establish his triumphant position with full deliberation. He sent Mæcenas and Agrippa to Italy, the one to govern the city, the other to control the legions in his absence; while he advanced in person into Greece, and thence into Asia, receiving on all sides the greetings of the people, and making arrangements for their future government. He returned to Italy in the course of the ensuing winter. Knights and senators, together with multitudes of citizens, came as far as Brundisium to meet him. He listened graciously to the complaints of his veterans, sold his own effects and those of his nearest friends to satisfy them, planted new colonies in the lands of conquered cities, and finally promised an ample donative from the anticipated spoil of Egypt. With the beginning of spring, B.C. 30, he was again in a condition to follow the track of the fugitives.

Despair of Antonius and Cleopatra at Alexandria.

To them six months' respite had been granted. We can hardly suppose that the court of Alexandria, even though swayed by the vigorous arms of a great Roman imperator, could present any effective resistance to the whole power of Rome, if once brought to bear against it. Yet Egypt abounded in wealth; she was the emporium of the immense trade which converged thither from both the Mediterranean and the Indian Ocean; she was one of the principal granaries of Rome and Italy; though her native population was feeble and unwarlike she could purchase the swords of the mercenary soldiers who swarmed on every side; her rulers were skilled in state craft, and could intrigue at least with all the discontented rulers and peoples, to whom their enforced submission to the great republic was ever odious. We cannot but think that chiefs of real spirit and resolution might have defended themselves under such circumstances against any power that could be arrayed against them. But it was not so. Antonius and Cleopatra traversed the sea in the same vessel. The Roman landed at Parætonium to secure the small garrison of the place; the Egyptian entered the port of Alexandria with laurels displayed on her deck for fear of the tumult which the sudden news of her disaster might awaken. There was neither love nor obedience awaiting her in her own capital. Her power rested on no popular foundation, and of this, she, as the descendant of a long line of foreign potentates, was no doubt well aware. Antonius himself was repulsed by a handful of Roman soldiers. The only relief for the despair which he began to entertain might be derived from the devotion, fruitless though it was, of a small band of gladiators who made their way through Asia and Syria to join him, and only yielded to Herod, king of Judæa, on the false assurance of their patron's death. Then it was that Cleopatra proposed to flee into Arabia; but her vessels were destroyed by the wild inhabitants of the Red Sea coast. Again the wretched pair contemplated an attempt to escape into Spain any quarter of the world seemed to them, in their cowardly distress, securer than their own dominion. When this scheme, too, was relinquished, Antonius shut himself up in a solitary tower. Cleopatra made show at least of greater resolution, and presented herself to the people in military costume, as if to animate them to resistance, but in private she abandoned herself together with her lover, who had crept back to her embraces, to her accustomed orgies, while she made experiments with various kinds of poison, and ascertained, it was said, that the most painless of deaths is that which follows on the bite of the asp.

Antonius kills himself.

The two helpless associates were not even true to one another. Each began to negotiate separately with the victor. To Antonius no answer was vouchsafed; better hopes were held out to Cleopatra if she would turn against her paramour. Octavius, ever cautious, even when the game was in his hands, and anxious to secure her person to embellish his future triumphs, continued to amuse and deceive her. He allowed his agents to remind her of his youth and of her own well-tried fascinations. When Antonius gained a trifling but useless advantage over the first battalion which the enemy threw on his shore, she deemed the time come to separate her interests from his, and treacherously induced his ships to abandon him. At the same moment, and perhaps through the same treachery, the last of his cohorts deserted him. The queen had shut herself up in a tower constructed for her mausoleum. Fearing the violence of the man she had ruined, she caused him to be assured that she had killed herself. With the infatuated renegade all was now over, and be determined himself to die. With the aid of his freed man, Eros, he gave himself a mortal wound; but while yet living he learnt that she, too, still survived, and causing himself thereupon to be brought to the foot of her tower, he was drawn up to her by her women, and there expired in her arms.

Death of Cleopatra.

Octavius at the same moment entered Alexandria. He charged an officer to secure the queen alive. Cleopatra refused him admittance; when he scaled her chamber she pretended to stab herself; he seized her arm and assured her of his master's kindness. At length she suffered herself to be removed to the palace, and there awaited an interview with the conqueror, prepared to exert all her charms upon him, with the bust of Cæsar presented to his view, but the attempted seduction proved fruitless, as might have been expected. Octavius kept, indeed, his eyes on the ground, but he never lost his coolness and self-possession. While she was flattering and caressing him, he coldly demanded a list of her treasures, which he required to be surrendered; but for herself he bade her be of good courage, and trust to his magnanimity. Cleopatra was soon made to understand that though her life should be spared, she would be removed to Rome and exhibited in the conqueror's triumph. She resolved to die. Retiring to the mausoleum where lay the body of Antonius, she crowned his bier with flowers, and was found the next morning dead on her couch her two women weeping beside her. "Is this well?" exclaimed the dismayed emissary of Octavius. "It is well," replied Charmion, "and worthy of the daughter of kings." The manner of her death was never certainly known. At the triumph, thus deprived of the ornament of her living presence her image was carried on a bier, the arms encircled by two serpents, which served to confirm the rumor that she had perished by the bite of an asp, brought to her, as was reported, in a basket of figs. The child of the foreign woman by Julius Cæsar was cruelly put to death, to appease the exaggerated or pretended sentiments of Roman nationality; while the offspring of Antonius and the matron Fulvia was suffered to survive and retain his birthright as a citizen. The dynasty of the Ptolemies ceased to reign. The Macedonian conquest was replaced by the Roman, and Egypt was finally reduced to the condition of a province. Octavius was master of the commonwealth, and became the founder of an empire.

Concluding remarks.

Between these two results there is a great difference to be noted. Marius and Pompeius had both been virtually masters of the commonwealth before Octavius; Sulla and Cæsar had been so actually, and had been confirmed as such by legal appointment. The first Triumvirate had dominated over it; the second had extorted from it supreme authority, and had demanded a renewal of its powers as long as its members could keep on terms of alliance one with another. The commonwealth had fallen under a succession of masters, and if from time to time it recovered a momentary independence, it was only by a fitful struggle, which showed its own intrinsic weakness and inability to rule itself. Rome might have fallen again and again into the hands of other masters, each wresting the sovereignty from his predecessor by force, and each yielding it in turn to a stronger successor. The body politic might have been torn in pieces, and either have been split into a number of states or perished in anarchy altogether. The barbarians of the Rhine and the Danube might have arrived three centuries before their time. But it was not to be so. Octavius founded an empire. Every age may produce many men who can destroy an empire, but rarely is the man born who can found one. It was the singular fortune of Rome—rather let us say, it was the special Providence which presides over all human history—that presented mankind, at this most critical epoch of their career, with the individual man who could actually perform the work required for the maintenance of the ancient civilization. In the overthrow of the so-called Roman liberty there is doubtless something to regret, but surely not much; for Roman liberty was little else than general servitude. In the violence and selfishness by which this overthrow was effected there is much which the moralist may be called upon to denounce, though, in view of the vastness of the issue involved, the historian will hardly pause to weigh nicely in the balance the crimes of one or other of the actors in the shifting scenes before him. The defects and sins of the empire which followed may be estimated by those who undertake specially to describe it; but the moral to be drawn from the epoch before us is this, that Rome had reached the moment when she could no longer retain her political liberty, and that the struggles of her Triumvirates could only end either in anarchy or in monarchy.

CHRONOLOGICAL TABLE.

U.C. 676. / B.C. 78. } Consuls { M. Æmilius Lepidus. / Q. Lutatius Catulus.

Death of Sulla. P. Servilius (consul 675) attacks the Cilician pirates. Progress of the war with Sertorius. The consul Lepidus conspires against the ruling party in the state.

U.C. 677. / B.C. 77. } Consuls { D. Junius Brutus. / M. Æmilius Lepidus.

Overthrow of M. Lepidus (consul 676). Pompeius sent against Sertorius.

U.C. 678. / B.C. 76. } Consuls { Cn. Octavius. / C Scribonius Curio.

Continuation of war with Sertorius. Sicinius fails in attempting to restore the Tribunician power.

U.C. 679. / B.C. 75. } Consuls { L. Octavius. / C. Aurelius Cotta.

Progress of the war with Sertorius. Servilius subdues the Isaurians. Cicero quæstor in Sicily.

U.C. 680. / B.C. 74. } Consuls { L. Licinius Lucullus. / M. Aurelius Cotta.

War with Sertorius. He refuses an alliance with Mithridates. Further attempt to rescind the Cornelian laws of Sulla.

U.C. 681. / B.C. 73. } Consuls { M. Terentius Varro. / C. Cassius Varus.

War with Sertorius. Mithridates defeated at Cyzicus by Lucullus. Insurrection of the gladiators under Spartacus.

| U.C. 682. B.C. 72. | Consuls | L. Gellius Poplicola.
Cn. Cornelius Lentulus. |

Sertorius assassinated, and the war brought to an end. Lucullus besieges Amisus. The consuls defeated by Spartacus.

| U.C. 683. B.C. 71. | Consuls | P. Cornelius Lentulus.
Cn Aufidius Orestes. |

Spartacus overthrown by Crassus. Progress of the Mithridatic war. Pompeius and Metellus triumph over Spain.

| U.C. 684. B.C. 70. | Consuls | Cn. Pompeius Magnus
M. Licinius Crasus Dives. |
| | Censors | L. Gellius Poplicola.
Cn. Cornelius Lentulus. |

Lucullus occupied with the internal administration of Asia Minor. The consuls restore the Tribunician power (lex Pompeia tribunicia). The Judicia are restored to the knights (lex Aurelia judiciaria). The process against Verres. Birth of the poet Virgil.

| U.C. 685. B.C. 69. | Consuls | Q. Hortensius.
Q. Cæcilius Metellus (Creticus). |

Lucullus makes war on Tigranes, king of Armenia. Catulus dedicates the temple of Jupiter. Capitolinus restored after the conflagration. U. C. 671. Cicero ædile.

| U.C. 686. B.C. 68. | Consuls | L. Cæcilius Metellus.
Q. Marcius Rex. |

Progress of the war in the East. Q. Metellus, consul (685) attacks the Cretans.

| U.C. 687. B.C. 67. | Consuls | C. Calpurnius Piso.
M. Acilius Glabrio. |

Mutiny in the army of Lucullus. Successes of Mithridates. Pompeius appointed to command against the Cilician pirates (lex Gabinia). Metellus finishes the war in Crete and obtains the sur name of Creticus. Cæsar questor in Spain.

| U.C. 688. B.C. 66. | Consuls | M. Æmilius Lepidus.
 L. Volcatius Tullus. |

Pompeius appointed to the command against Mithridates (lex Manilia). Cicero prætor.

| U.C. 689. B.C. 65. | Consuls | L. Aurelius Cotta.
 L. Manlius Torquatus. |
| | Censors | Q. Lutatius Catulus.
 M. Licinius Crassus Dives. |

Campaign of Pompeius against the Albani and Iberi. Abortive schemes of Catilina. Cæsar ædile. Birth of the poet Horace.

| U.C. 690. B.C. 64. | Consuls | L. Julius Cæsar.
 C. Marcius Figulus. |

Pompeius annexes Syria as a province. Cicero a candidate for the consulship, together with Catilina.

| U.C. 691. B.C. 63. | Consuls | M. Tullius Cicero.
 C. Antonius. |

Death of Mithridates. Pompeius subdues Palestine and Phœnicia. The conspiracy of Catilina defeated by Cicero, and his associates put to death. Birth of C. Octavius, afterwards the Emperor Augustus.

| U.C. 692. B.C. 62. | Consuls | D. Junius Silanus.
 L. Licinius Murena. |

Defeat and death of Catilina. Cæsar prætor and pontifex maximus. Cato tribune.

| U.C. 693. B.C. 61. | Consuls | M. Pupius Piso.
 M. Valerius Messala. |

Pompeius returns to Rome and triumphs. Process and acquittal of Clodius.

| U.C. 694. B.C. 60. | Consuls | L. Africanius.
 Q. Cæcilius Metellus Celer. |

Cæsar proprætor in Further Spain. The senate refuses to ratify the acts of Pompeius. Agrarian measure of the tribune Flavius. Disturbances in the city. Pompeius, Cæsar, and Crassus form an alliance; the First Triumvirate.

| U.C. 695. B.C. 59. | Consuls | C. JULIUS CÆSAR. M. CALPURNIUS BIBULUS. |

The leges Juliæ: 1. for relief of the publicani in Asia; 2. for division of lands in Campania. Acts of Pompeius confirmed through Cæsar's influence. The Gaulish and Illyricum assigned provinces to Cæsar. Birth of the historian Livy.

| U.C. 696. B.C. 58. | Consuls | L. CALPURNIUS PISO. A. GABINIUS. |

Cæsar proconsul in Gaul. First year of the Gallic war. Defeat of the Helvetii and Suevi. Tribunate of Clodius. Banishment of Cicero. Cato sent to Cyprus.

| U.C. 697. B.C. 57. | Consuls | P. CORNELIUS LENTULUS SPINTHER. Q. CÆCILIUS METELLUS NEPOS. |

Second year of the Gallic war. Cæsar subdues the Belgian tribes. Victory over the Nervii. Cicero recalled from banishment.

| U.C. 698. B.C. 56. | Consuls | C. CORNELIUS LENTULUS MARCELLINUS. L. MARCIUS PHILIPPUS. |

Third year of the Gallic war. Cæsar subdues the Veneti. Subjugation of the west and south of Gaul. The triumvirs meet at the end of the year at Lucca. Cato returns from Cyprus.

| U.C. 699. B.C. 55. | Consuls | CN. POMPEIUS MAGNUS II. M. LICINIUS CRASSUS II. |
| | Censors | M. VALERIUS MESSALA. P. SERVILIUS ISAURICUS. |

Fourth year of the Gallic war. Cæsar crosses the Rhine and invades Britain. Gabinius restores Ptolemæus Auletes to the throne of Egypt. Pompeius completes and dedicates his theatre at Rome.

| U.C. 700. B.C. 54. | Consuls | L. DOMITIUS AHENOBARBUS. APP. CLAUDIUS PULCHER. |

Fifth year of the Gallic war. Cæsar's second invasion of Britain. Revolt of the Belgian tribes; destruction of Sabinus and Cotta with their armies. Crassus proconsul in Syria. Process of Gabinius. Death of Julia. Cato prætor.

| U.C. 701. | Consuls | Cn. Domitius Calvinus. |
| B.C. 53. | | M. Valerius Messala. |

Sixth year of the Gallic war. Campaign in Belgica and destruction of the Eburones. Expedition of Crassus against the Parthians. Battle of Carrhæ. His defeat and death.

| U.C. 702. | Consuls | Cn. Pompeius Magnus III. (without a colleague.) |
| B.C. 52. | | Q. Cæcil Metellus Pius Scipio (in the last half of the year). |

Seventh year of the Gallic war. Revolt of the Gauls under Vercingetorix. Battle of Alesia. Clodius assassinated. Process of Milo. Death of the poet Lucretius.

| U.C. 703. | Consuls | Serv. Sulpicius Rufus. |
| B.C. 51. | | M. Claudius Marcellus. |

Eighth year of the Gallic war. Final pacification of Gaul. Cicero proconsul in Cilicia.

U.C. 704.	Consuls	L. Æmilius Paulus.
B.C. 50.		C. Claudius Marcellus.
	Censors	App. Claudius Pulcher.
		L. Calpurnius Piso.

Cæsar regulates the province of Gaul. The senate requires him to surrender his command. Sickness and recovery of Pompeius. Tribunate of Curio; imminence of civil war.

U.C. 705.	Consuls	C. Claudius Marcellus.
B.C. 49.		L. Cornelius Lentulus Crus
	Dictator	C. Julius Cæsar.

Outbreak of the civil war. Cæsar crosses the Rubicon. Pompeius evacuates Italy. Cæsar reduces the legions in Spain and takes Massilia. He is created dictator. Defeat and death of Curio in Africa.

| U.C. 706. | Consuls | C. Julius Cæsar II. |
| B.C. 48. | | P. Servilius Isauricus. |

Cæsar's campaign in Epirus. Battle of Pharsalia. Flight of Pompeius and his assassination in Egypt. Cæsar lands at Alexandria, and supports Cleopatra against Ptolemæus.

U.C. 707. B.C. 47.	Consuls	Q. Fufius Calenus. P. Vatinius.
	Dictator	C. Julius Cæsar II.

Cæsar's warfare at Alexandria. Death of Ptolemæus. Restoration of Cleopatra. Cæsar makes war upon Pharnaces. Battle of Zela. Cæsar returns to Rome, and thence transports his forces into Africa.

U.C. 708. B.C. 46.	Consuls	C. Julius Cæsar III. M. Æmilius Lepidus.
	Dictator	C. Julius Cæsar III.

The war in Africa. Battle of Thapsus. Death of Cato at Utica. Cæsar pursues the younger Cn. Pompeius in Spain. Cæsar's legislation at Rome (leges Juliæ). Correction of the Calendar.

U.C. 709. B.C. 45.	Consuls	C. Julius Cæsar IV. Q. Fabius Maximus. C. Caninius Rebilus.
	Dictator	C. Julius Cæsar IV.

Defeat and death of Cn. Pompeius. Cæsar triumphs. Complete establishment of his power. First year of the Julian Calendar.

U.C. 710. B.C. 44.	Consuls	C. Julius Cæsar V. M. Antonius. P. Cornelius Dolabella Suffect
	Dictator	C. Julius Cæsar V.

Cæsar assassinated. Intrigues of Antonius. Disturbances at Cæsar's funeral. Flight of the Liberators. Octavius assumes Cæsar's inheritance. Preparations for war.

U.C. 711. B.C. 43	Consuls	C. Vibius Pansa. A. Hirtius. C. Julius Cæsar Octavianus (Octavius). Q. Pedius. C. Carrinas. } Suffect. P. Ventidius.

Cicero's activity at Rome. Battles before Mutina and deaths of Hirtius and Pansa. Octavius unites with M. Antonius and Lepidus. The Second Triumvirate. Proscription and death of Cicero.

| U.C. 712. B.C. 42 | Consuls | L. Munatius Plancus.
M. Æmilius Lepidus II. |

Octavius and Antonius encounter the Republicans in the East. Battle of Philippi. Death of Brutus and Cassius.

| U.C. 714. B.C. 40. | Consuls | Cn. Domitius Calvinus II.
C. Asinius Pollio.
C. Cornelius Balbus — Suffect.
P. Caninidius Crassus — Suffect. |

Antonius quits Alexandria. Death of Fulvia and treaty of Brundisium. Marriage of Antonius with Octavia. The Triumvirs make war upon Sextus Pompeius.

| U.C. 715. B.C. 39. | Consuls | L. Marcius Censorinus.
C. Calvisius Sabinus. |

The treaty of Misenum. Octavius and Antonius at Rome. Octavius in Gaul. Antonius at Athens. Ventidius defeats the Parthians.

| U.C. 716. B.C. 38. | Consuls | App. Claudius Pulcher.
C. Norbanus Flaccus. |

The Sicilian war. Antonius in the East. The Triumvirate prolonged.

| U.C. 717. B.C. 37. | Consuls | M. Vipsanius Agrippa.
L. Caninius Gallus.
T. Statilius Taurus, Suffect. |

Continuation of the Sicilian war. Octavius and Antonius meet at Tarentum. Naval force of Octavius and construction of the Portus Julius.

| U.C. 718. B.C. 36. | Consuls | L. Gellius Poplicola.
L. Munatius Plancus, Suffect.
M. Cocceius Nerva. |

End of the Sicilian war. Overthrow and flight of Sextus Pompeius. Fall of Lepidus, the triumvir. Disasters of Antonius in Parthia.

U.C. 719.	Consuls	L. Cornificius.
B.C. 35.		Sextus Pompeius
		(not the son of Pompeius Magnus).

Octavius fights in the Alps and in Illyricum. Sextus Pompeius slain in Asia. Antonius resides with Cleopatra at Alexandria. He forbids Octavia to come to him.

U.C. 720.	Consuls	L. Scribonius Libo.
B.C. 34.		M. Antonius II.
		L. Sempronius Atratinus, Suffect.

Octavius subdues the Dalmatians. Antonius captures Artavasdes king of Armenia, and celebrates a triumph in Alexandria.

U.C. 721.	Consuls	C. Julius Cæsar Octavianus II.
B.C. 33.		P. Autronius Pœtus, Suffectus.
		L. Volcatius Tullus.

Third campaign of Octavius in Illyricum. Antonius at Alexandria.

| U.C. 722. | Consuls | Cn. Domitius Ahenobarbus. |
| B.C. 32. | | C. Sosius. |

Rupture between Octavius and Antonius. Preparation for war. Antonius at Samos.

| U.C. 723. | Consuls | C. Julius Cæsar Octavianus III. |
| B.C. 31. | | M. Valerius Messala Corvinus. |

Battle of Actium. Flight of Antonius and Cleopatra to Egypt.

| U.C. 724. | Consuls | C. Julius Cæsar Octavianus IV. |
| B.C. 30. | | M. Licinius Crassus. |

Octavius reaches Egypt in pursuit. Death of Antonius and Cleopatra. Egypt annexed to the Roman Empire. Undisputed ascendency of Octavius.